T0179722

Perentie

Jackson's chameleon

THE ULTIMATE BOOK OF REPTILES

YOUR GUIDE TO THE SECRET LIVES OF THESE SCALY, SLITHERY, AND SPECTACULAR CREATURES

RUCHIRA SOMAWEERA WITH
STEPHANIE WARREN DRIMMER

NATIONAL GEOGRAPHIC
Washington, D.C.

CONTENTS

Leopard gecko

Green turtle

Satanic leaf-tailed gecko

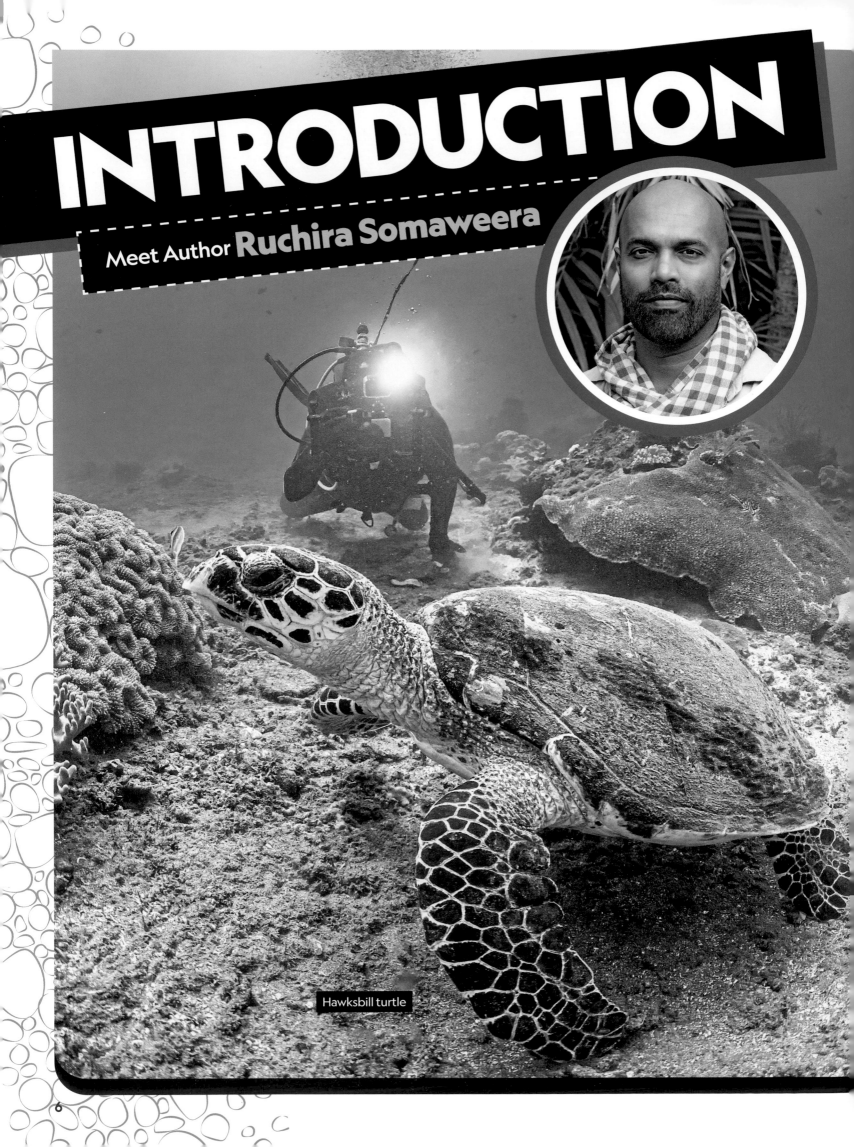

INTRODUCTION

Meet Author **Ruchira Somaweera**

Hawksbill turtle

Komodo dragon

Blue Malaysian coral snake

I'VE BEEN CHASING REPTILES SINCE I WAS A LITTLE KID GROWING UP IN THE TROPICAL ISLAND OF SRI LANKA.

I was lucky: Sri Lanka is a world hot spot for reptiles. It's home to many species, from bright green dragon lizards to colorful star tortoises, to over 100 different types of snakes. I loved all sorts of animals growing up, but especially reptiles. I saw reptiles as neglected animals that many people hardly get to know. Most people think reptiles are scary, or ugly, or slimy. But I think they are amazing, mesmerizing, and beautiful!

I went on to become a herpetologist: a scientist who studies reptiles. I spend a lot of my time doing field research, or going out and studying reptiles in their natural habitats. That has brought me to some incredible places. I've seen the flying lizards and snakes in the rainforest of Borneo, and green geckos and the primitive tuatara in New Zealand. I've been to Komodo island many times, and once I stepped on a sleeping Komodo dragon! In Africa, I've spotted black mambas and puff adders, often considered Africa's most dangerous snakes.

Along the way, I've learned all kinds of new things about how reptiles live. Very little is known about most reptiles—even by experts! We're still in the dark about the basics for most reptiles, like how they reproduce, what environmental conditions they need to survive, or even how many there are. And as we go into the wild to study reptiles, we are not only discovering new information, but new species. We find hundreds of new-to-science species every year!

Reptiles are an incredible group of animals to get to know. And knowing them is extremely important because reptiles play a huge role in maintaining a balanced environment to keep the planet healthy. They are also highly valuable in medical research, and they control pests, too. But many reptiles are being hit hard by human impacts such as deforestation, overharvesting, and climate change. It's more important than ever before that we respect and celebrate the world of reptiles— and show people that they're far more than just scaly and slithering creatures!

American alligator

Indian star tortoise

Komodo dragon

Madagascar
giant day gecko

CHAPTER ONE

REPTILES
IN THE
WILD

Eyelash palm pit viper

>>> THEY LURK IN CORNERS AND CREVICES, WAITING TO STRIKE. THEY SLITHER AND HISS AND SNAP WITH SHARP TEETH. THEY'RE SCALY AND THEY'RE DEFINITELY SCARY ... AREN'T THEY? WELL, NOT QUITE. Reptiles are an enormous group of animals, with nearly 12,000 species that make their home alongside us on planet Earth. Some reptiles weigh more than a small car, and some are so tiny they could balance on a fingertip. Some reptiles live deep underground, some glide through the air—and some even run on water! Some use camouflage to nearly disappear into their surroundings. Others change their color at will to show off.

Yet many of these amazing abilities go unnoticed. That's because reptiles are perhaps the most misunderstood group of creatures on the planet. But you can help begin to change that. Turn the page to discover the world of reptiles, in all their scaly, slithering glory. One thing's for certain: You're sure to be surprised!

WHAT IS A REPTILE?

Tyrannosaurus rex

Quick quiz! Which animal is a reptile?

A. Veiled chameleon
B. Indian star tortoise
C. Tyrannosaurus rex
D. All of the above

If you answered D, you're right! Though some people might think of reptiles as just snakes and lizards, the group actually includes a whole variety of animals, including turtles, something called a tuatara, and yes, even dinosaurs!

Indian star tortoise

Emerald boa

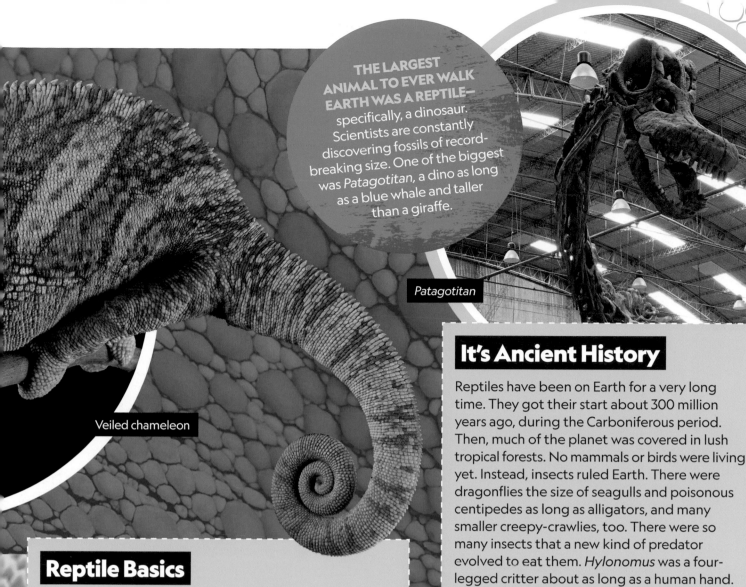

THE LARGEST ANIMAL TO EVER WALK EARTH WAS A REPTILE—specifically, a dinosaur. Scientists are constantly discovering fossils of record-breaking size. One of the biggest was *Patagotitan*, a dino as long as a blue whale and taller than a giraffe.

Patagotitan

Veiled chameleon

Reptile Basics

Reptiles have skins covered with plates called scales. They have a backbone, like birds and mice and you (and not like insects, which have a hard outer body covering instead). They mostly breathe air, using lungs (and not like amphibians, which breathe through their skin as well as through their lungs and gills). Most reptiles survive by eating other animals, and they lay hard-shelled eggs on land. They include snakes, lizards, tortoises, turtles, crocodiles, and alligators.

What a Scramble

Birds lay eggs. Most mammals give birth to live babies. But what about reptiles? These creatures use a mix of strategies when it comes to making young. Most snakes, lizards, crocodiles, and turtles lay shelled eggs like birds do. A few snakes produce eggs, but they hold them inside their bodies until the eggs hatch and the young exit their mother's body. Some lizards and snakes give birth to live young, like humans do.

Sea turtle eggs

It's Ancient History

Reptiles have been on Earth for a very long time. They got their start about 300 million years ago, during the Carboniferous period. Then, much of the planet was covered in lush tropical forests. No mammals or birds were living yet. Instead, insects ruled Earth. There were dragonflies the size of seagulls and poisonous centipedes as long as alligators, and many smaller creepy-crawlies, too. There were so many insects that a new kind of predator evolved to eat them. *Hylonomus* was a four-legged critter about as long as a human hand. And it was one of the earliest reptiles to walk the planet.

As time went on, reptiles exploded into many different species. Three different reptile groups emerged: The anapsid group includes modern-day turtles and tortoises. The synapsids include a family line that eventually became the first mammals. And the diapsids split into many new subgroups, including crocodiles, flying reptiles, and dinosaurs.

The dinosaurs evolved into hundreds of species. Some ate plants. Others ate meat. Some were small. Others grew to such enormous size that they became the biggest animals to ever walk the land. They dominated the planet until about 66 million years ago, when a giant asteroid slammed into Earth and the dinosaurs were wiped out, along with about 75 percent of other species. But one kind of dinosaur survived: flying feathered creatures that still inhabit our skies today. We call them birds. Today, birds are some of the only living members left of the diapsids—along with all other living reptiles, from crocodiles to snakes to lizards.

GREEN ANACONDA

>>> **POUND FOR POUND, THE GREEN ANACONDA IS THE LARGEST SNAKE IN THE WORLD.** It can weigh as much as an adult male tiger at 550 pounds (250 kg). It can also grow longer than six 10-year-olds lying head to foot!

On land, this snake is a clumsy mover. But the green anaconda is semiaquatic, meaning it inhabits both land and water. When it enters a swamp, marsh, or stream, it becomes a quick and stealthy hunter. It spends much of its time lying nearly submerged, with just its eyes and nose poking out above the water's surface. There, it waits until a tasty wild pig, deer, capybara, or even a jaguar or a caiman wanders by. Then it strikes. Anacondas don't have a venomous bite. Instead, they kill their prey by constriction, coiling their muscular bodies around the animal and squeezing until it runs out of air.

WHERE IT'S FOUND: Rainforests and wetlands in South America, especially in the Orinoco and Amazon Basins

FUN FACT: Anacondas stretch their jaws wide to swallow their prey whole.

WHERE IT'S FOUND:
Galápagos Islands

FUN FACT: There were once so many Galápagos tortoises that the islands are named after them—the Spanish word for "tortoise" is *galápago*.

GALÁPAGOS TORTOISE

>>> TWO OR THREE MILLION YEARS AGO, TORTOISES FROM SOUTH AMERICA WASHED UP ON THE SHORES OF THE GALÁPAGOS ISLANDS, A GROUP OF VOLCANO-CREATED ISLANDS ABOUT 600 MILES (966 KM) OFF THE COAST OF ECUADOR. There, over many generations, the tortoises grew enormous in size. Today, they are the world's largest tortoise, with some individuals growing more than five feet (1.5 m) long and weighing more than 500 pounds (227 kg)— as much as an adult black bear!

Galápagos tortoises spend their lives snacking on grasses, leaves, and cacti. When they're not eating, they're resting—they can sleep for nearly 16 hours a day! A slow-paced lifestyle, plus an ability to store food and water for long periods of time, means that these tortoises can go up to a year without eating or drinking.

NILE CROCODILE

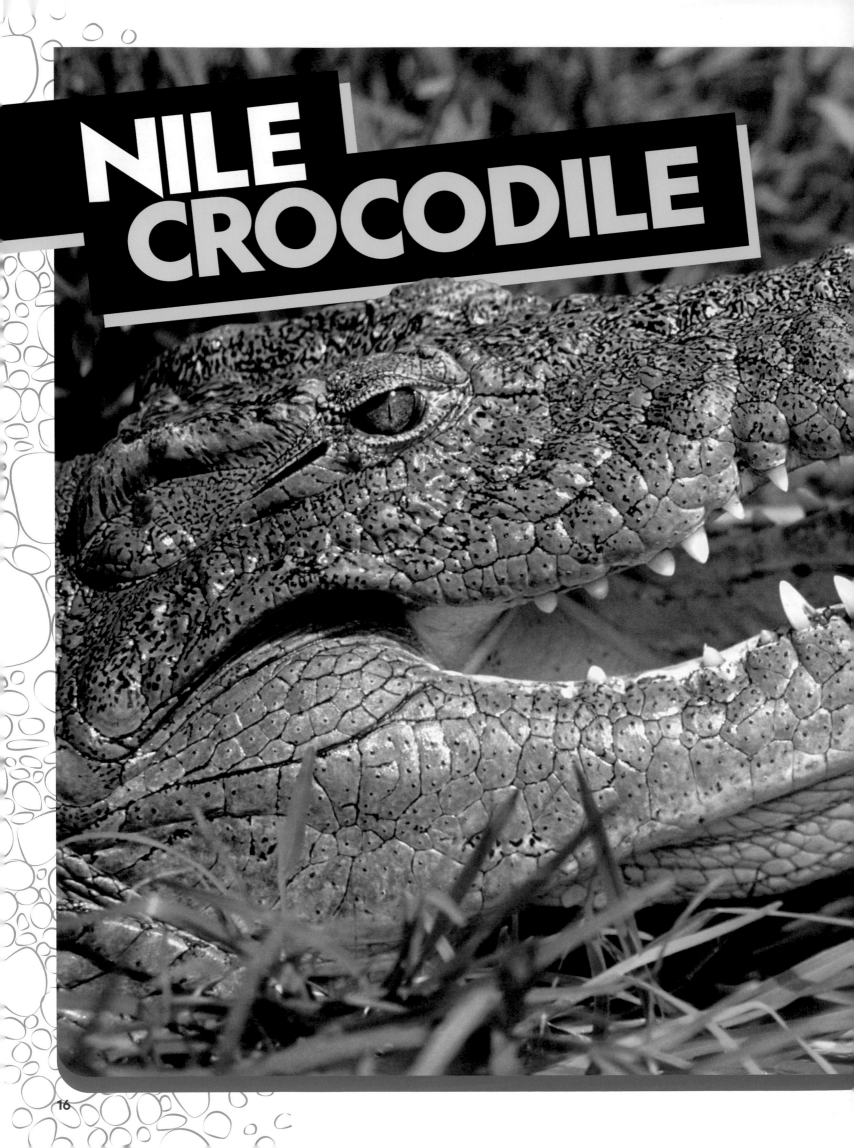

>>> **DESPITE THEIR ENORMOUS SIZE, NILE CROCODILES EAT MOSTLY FISH AND CRABS.** But occasionally, they will attack almost anything that crosses their path, from porcupines to zebras to other crocodiles. People sometimes call Nile crocodiles one of the planet's most dangerous animals. That's because these reptiles do attack people who have to share their waters for bathing, fishing, and other activities.

For such powerful predators, Nile crocodiles are surprisingly gentle parents. After a female crocodile lays up to 80 eggs, she will guard the nest for three months, and the male will often stand guard close by as well. When the babies are born, the female crocodile protects them for as long as two years, until they are big enough to fend for themselves.

WHERE IT'S FOUND: Rivers, lakes, freshwater marshes, and mangrove swamps in sub-Saharan Africa, the Nile Basin, and Madagascar

FUN FACT: A Nile crocodile can weigh more than a cow.

REPTILE BITES

Early reptiles dominated Earth for about
180 MILLION YEARS.

THERE ARE ABOUT 4,000 SPECIES OF SNAKES—
but only about 600 are venomous, and only 200 have enough venom to seriously harm a human.

About one in every five reptile species is
THREATENED WITH EXTINCTION.

Open wide! Almost all snakes
SWALLOW THEIR FOOD WHOLE.

The earliest known reptile ancestor, *Hylonomus lyelli*, looked much like a modern lizard—but it **LIVED 315 MILLION YEARS AGO!**

There are more than **7,000 SPECIES OF LIZARDS** on Earth.

Some reptiles eat plants, some eat animals, and **SOME EAT CARRION** (dead animals).

Reptiles live on every continent **EXCEPT ANTARCTICA—** it's too cold for them there.

GILA MONSTER

WHERE IT'S FOUND: Deserts of the southwestern United States and northwestern Mexico

FUN FACT: The Gila monster is the largest lizard native to the United States.

>>> **IT'S NOT A MONSTER.** But it is one of the few venomous lizards in the world. The Gila (HEE-luh) monster has venom about as toxic as that of a diamondback rattlesnake. But instead of injecting venom into its victim like a snake does, the Gila monster latches on and chews, causing its toxins to move into the prey's wound through grooves in its teeth. Because it can only dispense limited venom this way, no Gila monster is known to have ever killed a human—though a bite from one is said to be incredibly painful!

Gila monsters may be venomous, but they are not aggressive. In fact, they spend more than 95 percent of their time resting in underground burrows. Like camels, which store fat in their humps, Gila monsters can store fat in their tails. If they need to, they can go months between meals by living off this food source.

KING COBRA

>>> **THIS SNAKE IS CALLED THE "KING" COBRA FOR A REASON: IT IS THE LARGEST AND LONGEST OF ALL HIGHLY VENOMOUS SNAKES IN THE WORLD.** Given its massive size, it can also inject a large amount of venom during a bite, making it a highly dangerous snake, too. It's ferocious enough to kill and eat other snakes, including other types of cobras. When a king cobra feels threatened, it will lift the upper part of its body off the ground, and expand ribs and muscles on both sides of its neck to create a "hood" that makes it look even bigger and tougher. If that's not enough to scare away an attacker, the cobra can also make a hissing sound that's similar to a dog's growl.

King cobras are certainly dangerous snakes. But other than nesting females, which can attack unprovoked, they only strike as a last resort, preferring to escape instead. King cobra venom is deadly enough to kill an elephant—but it's useful, too. Scientists studying the venom have been able to use what they've learned to create several powerful pain medications.

WHERE IT'S FOUND: Mainly rainforests and plains of South and Southeast Asia

FUN FACT: King cobras are about twice as long as a typical NBA basketball player is tall.

>>> **GECKOS ARE KNOWN FOR THEIR INCREDIBLE ABILITY TO STICK TO SURFACES—EVEN WHEN VERTICAL OR UPSIDE DOWN.** But the tokay gecko has an especially impressive grip. Geckos get their cling power from toes covered in millions of fine, branching "hairs" too small to see with the naked eye. (Each foot has half a million hairs!) These hairs bond to the tiny molecules that make up a wall, ceiling, or tree, giving the gecko incredible sticking power. The tokay gecko's grip is so strong that it can grasp on to a vertical surface using a single toe!

Tokay geckos have a pattern of spots that they can lighten or darken to better blend in with their environment. They also have a fold of skin that they unfurl when resting on a tree. That blurs the line between lizard and bark, making the lizard's shadow look like part of the tree.

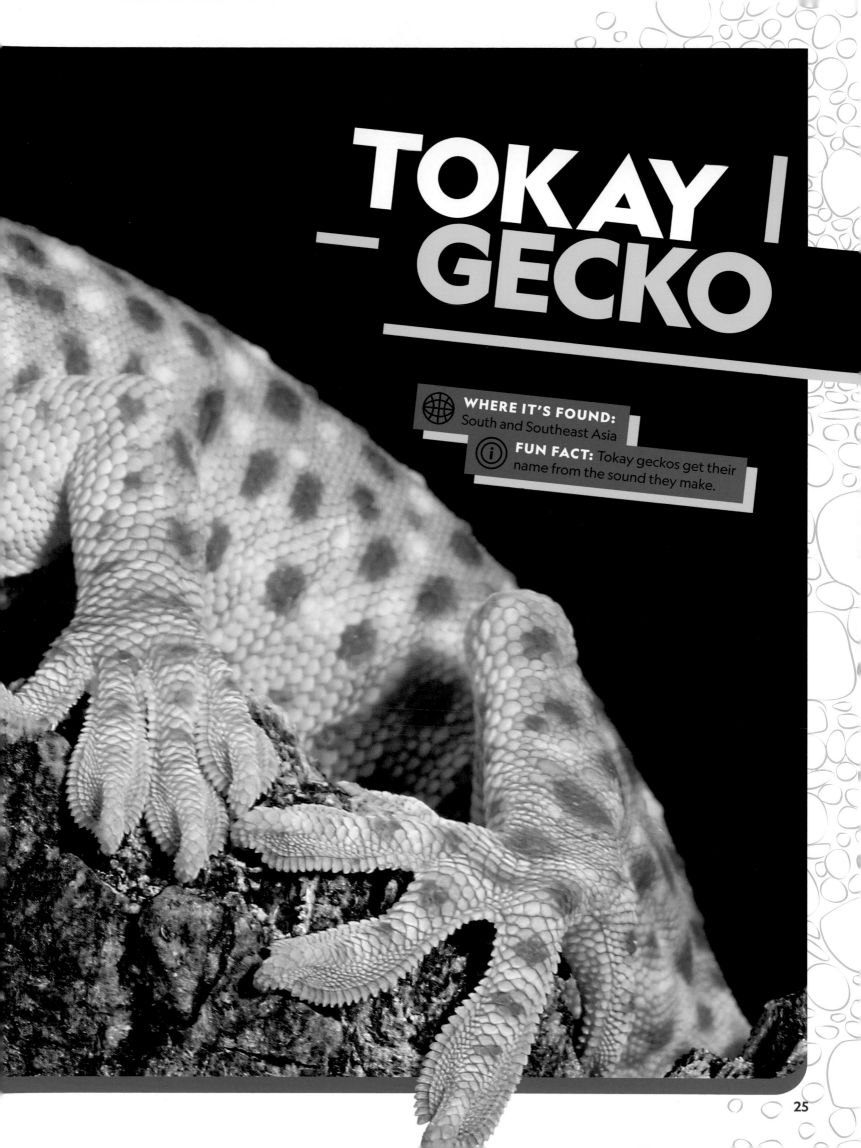

TOKAY GECKO

WHERE IT'S FOUND: South and Southeast Asia

FUN FACT: Tokay geckos get their name from the sound they make.

Moment of AHA!!!

"Normally, Sri Lankan hump-nosed lizards are a bit dull looking, which helps them blend in with the dark forest. So I was thrilled to see this very colorful specimen! This lizard also clearly showed every ornamentation these lizards have: a 'hump,' or rostral appendage on its snout, horns coming out of its head, a fold of skin called a dewlap below its chin, and a crest on its neck, along with the amazing colors. When it saw me, it hissed and opened its mouth to show the bright red inside—a typical threat display for this species."

—Ru Somaweera

LEATHERBACK TURTLE

WHERE IT'S FOUND: Ocean waters worldwide, except near poles

FUN FACT: Leatherbacks are the deepest-diving reptiles in the world, known to go deeper than 4,000 feet (1,220 m).

>>> **THIS OCEAN GIANT DOES THINGS DIFFERENTLY FROM OTHER REPTILES.** It is the only living member of an ancient turtle family that can trace its beginnings back more than 100 million years. Instead of scales and a hard shell, it has tough, rubbery skin—the trait that gives this turtle its name. It is also truly enormous, with some individuals weighing as much as 1,984 pounds (900 kg)—more than most horses!

Like other reptiles, leatherbacks are ectothermic, or "cold-blooded." But when they need to, they can also generate their own body heat like an endothermic, or "warm-blooded," animal. This ability means that leatherbacks can keep warm even in cold waters, giving them the ability to cruise most of Earth's oceans. Leatherbacks undertake the longest migration of any sea turtle, averaging 7,400 miles (11,900 km) round-trip. That's like crossing the continental United States two and a half times!

FRILLED LIZARD

>>> WHEN THIS LIZARD IS ALARMED, IT DOES SOME-THING STRANGE: IT RISES UP ON ITS HIND LEGS, OPENS ITS YELLOW MOUTH WIDE, AND UNFURLS A RUFF OF BRIGHT ORANGE, SCALY SKIN AROUND ITS NECK.

No wonder it's often called the frilled dragon in its homeland of Australia! The frilled lizard puts on a frightening display. But it's all for show: If its foe doesn't back down, this reptile turns tail and runs away on its back legs, its mouth and frill hanging open. It won't stop or look back until it reaches the safety of a tree. Trees are where frilled lizards spend most of their days, only coming down to the ground on occasion to snack on ants, termites, and small lizards—that is, until something scares them!

 WHERE IT'S FOUND: Forests and woodlands in northern Australia and southern New Guinea

 FUN FACT: The creators of *Jurassic Park* were inspired by the frilled lizard when they dreamed up how the dinosaur *Dilophosaurus* would look. But scientists don't know if *Dilophosaurus* had a frill in real life.

TUATARA

›› IT MIGHT LOOK LIKE A LIZARD, BUT THE TUATARA ISN'T ONE AT ALL. Instead, it's the only living member of a group of reptiles as old as the first dinosaurs. The tuatara is unlike any other reptile. For example, it likes cool weather, and it has odd jaws with two rows of upper teeth and a single row of lower teeth that fits snugly between them. That allows it to snap the heads right off its victims.

Strangest of all, the tuatara has a third eye on top of its head! The eye is visible at birth but later becomes covered with pigment and scales. The eye isn't used for seeing, but it is able to sense changes in light. Many lizards have a hidden third eye, called a parietal eye, but the tuatara's is highly developed. Scientists aren't totally sure of its purpose—but they suspect it acts like a calendar, letting the brain know that seasons are changing by tracking when days get longer and nights get shorter, and the reverse.

WHERE IT'S FOUND:
New Zealand

FUN FACT: Tuataras can live to be 100 years old.

›» IS IT A GIANT EARTHWORM?

No, it's an animal that's stranger still: a worm lizard. There are about 170 species of worm lizards, called amphisbaenians (am-fizz-BAY-nee-ans), a unique group of reptiles. Like earthworms, worm lizards burrow underground, moving through soil with the help of scales arranged in a ringlike pattern. Most are legless, though some have a pair of clawed front legs for digging. The red worm lizard is one of the biggest worm lizards, growing as long as a sidewinder rattlesnake.

Red worm lizards often live in the underground burrows of leafcutter ants, and don't seem to notice the ants' bites and stings. When threatened, they will curve into a horseshoe position with their tail and mouth raised. Because both ends look almost identical, this has led some people to call it the "two-headed snake"!

RED WORM LIZARD

WHERE IT'S FOUND:
South America, Trinidad, and Panama

FUN FACT: Snakes are the red worm lizard's major predator.

FACE-TO-FACE

WITH A BLUE MALAYSIAN CORAL SNAKE

IT HAS ALWAYS BEEN ONE OF MY DREAMS TO WORK IN BORNEO, KNOWN MOST FAMOUSLY FOR ITS ORANGUTANS AND ITS HORNBILLS, BIRDS THAT LOOK SIMILAR TO TOUCANS. But Borneo is also a world hot spot when it comes to reptiles.

I first got the chance to go to this island in 2006, and I immediately fell in love with it. Being a tropical island, it has its challenges. It's humid, it's hot, and there are so many bloodsucking leeches and insects. It's not an easy place to work. But it's extremely rewarding, because so much life comes out of the rainforest.

On this particular night, I was out with a team looking for geckos and frogs. But we found something else instead: a Malaysian striped coral snake. It was half dead, and we could see some bite marks where it looked like a bigger reptile had attacked it. Then, about 30 feet (10 m) away, we saw this bright object. It was a blue Malaysian coral snake. That's the first time any of us had ever seen one. They are absolutely beautiful, highly venomous, and we know very little about their behavior in the wild.

I picked up the snake to take a photo for our records and to get a genetic sample, which we do by cutting off a very small bit of the tip of the snake's tail. This snake bites only rarely. But I was still extremely careful when I did this, because if you were to get bitten deep in the Bornean jungle, you would be in trouble. You'd have to walk more than a mile (2 km) just to get to the road, and then to get to the nearest hospital would sometimes take days. Even if you made it, they likely would not have the correct antivenom to treat you, as not all hospitals store antivenom. But the risk was worth it: Getting the chance to see this rare, secretive snake— and document it for science—was amazing.

Marine iguana

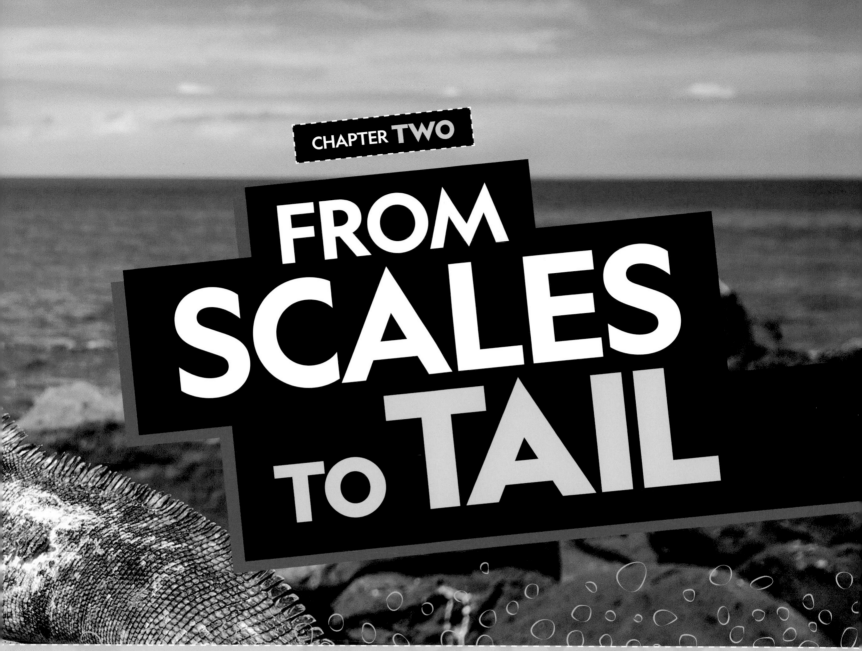

CHAPTER TWO

FROM SCALES TO TAIL

>>> **FROM SLITHERING SNAKES TO SHARP-TOOTHED CROCODILES TO LUMBERING TORTOISES, REPTILES TAKE MANY DIFFERENT FORMS.** They also survive in a variety of ways: Some are vegetarians and others are hunters. Some are desert dwellers and others live only in rainforests. Some defend themselves with tough shells and others go on the offensive with venomous bites.

Despite their differences, all reptiles share a set of traits they inherited from their ancestors, like backbones and scaly skin. All breathe air. And all depend on the sun to warm their bodies.

CREATURE FEATURES

Nostrils

Although amphibians, such as frogs, can absorb oxygen through their skin, reptiles must breathe air, like mammals and birds do. Even reptiles that spend their lives in the water, such as sea turtles and sea snakes, have to come to the surface to breathe.

Chameleon

Tongue

Snakes and some lizards smell using their tongues and a special organ in their mouth, called the Jacobson's organ. The forked tongue of many reptiles allows them to "catch" scent particles from air and direct them toward the Jacobson's organ.

Komodo dragon tongue

Legs

The ancestor of all reptiles had four legs. So most reptiles have four legs, too. Even in snakes, which have evolved over millions of years to lose their legs, certain species still have the tiny remains of leg bones in their skeletons. These bones can be seen with an x-ray.

Skin

Reptiles have a built-in suit of armor: their scales. Tough and waterproof, scales protect reptiles from predators and the environment—hot conditions, for example.

THE SKINNY ON SCALES

Most reptiles have skin totally or partially covered with hard scales. These scales are made of keratin, the same substance that forms your fingernails. These scales protect the reptile like a suit of armor. Also like a suit of armor, they have areas of thinner skin in between them. That allows the reptile's skin to bend and flex. Some reptiles, such as turtles, have two large bony plates: a carapace on top and a plastron on bottom, along with scales on their exposed body parts, such as the legs and tail.

While you will stop growing when you reach adulthood, reptiles can keep growing until they die. As they get bigger, they will periodically outgrow their outer layer. When that happens, reptiles shed their skin and replace it with the next size up. Lizards, turtles, and tortoises shed in patches. But snakes can shed their skin all at once (because they don't have legs or shells to get in the way), and sometimes they leave behind an inside-out snake skin!

Viper skin

Tail

Many reptiles have a long tail. Some use their tail like an extra limb, to hold on to branches when climbing a tree. Others use their tail to help propel them forward. And some can even shed their tail in self-defense.

MOST SNAKES HAVE FLAT, WIDE SCALES ON THEIR BELLIES CALLED SCUTES. They act like tire treads, helping the snake slither and grasp the surface. The scutes are attached to muscles that allow them to be tilted outward and pulled inward. This motion pushes the snake along the ground.

BLENDING IN AND STANDING OUT

Many reptiles come in shades of green and brown. But others can be every color of the rainbow, from blue to orange to hot pink. That's because some reptiles use their body colors to help them blend into the background. But other reptiles have a different tactic: They use bold color to say either "Look at me!" or "Don't even think of eating me!"

Reptiles are able to change color by **SHIFTING PIGMENT IN DIFFERENT LAYERS OF THEIR SKIN.**

Presto Chango

Internet videos show chameleons shifting from bright blue to neon purple to bold orange to match nearby objects—but these videos are fake! Chameleons are some of nature's most skilled color changers. Though they can make small adjustments to their color to better blend into their surroundings, chameleons such as the panther chameleon (p. 70) perform dramatic color changes for a different reason—to defend their territory and attract females.

Catching Rays

Many reptiles can shift their colors to stay at the ideal body temperature. If a green iguana gets too cold, for example, it will turn a shade of darker green. Because dark colors absorb more sunlight, this color change will help the iguana collect more of the sun's warmth. If the iguana gets too warm, it will turn a shade of paler green. Because light colors reflect sunlight away, that keeps the lizard from overheating.

Hiding Out

Slithering among leaf litter on the forest floor, the Gaboon viper is almost impossible to see. Even its wide head looks just like a fallen leaf, right down to the line through its middle that mimics a stem. That crafty camouflage helps the viper hide in plain sight, waiting for a tasty rodent or bird to come close. Then it strikes.

Disappearing Act

Some animals survive by looking scary and intimidating. Others disguise themselves as more dangerous creatures, and still others survive by making themselves invisible. That's the strategy of the Madagascan mossy leaf-tailed gecko. It looks exactly like the tree branches it likes to cling to—down to the spots of "moss" on its skin!

STAY BACK!

A rattlesnake's rattle and a cobra's hiss are warnings: "Stop right there, or I'll strike!" They are among the 600 or so species of venomous snakes. These reptiles are equipped with long front fangs that are hollow like needles. When a snake bites, its fangs inject toxic venom into its victims.

Turning Toxic

As you chew and swallow your food, special organs called salivary glands squirt saliva into your mouth. This saliva is laced with chemicals called enzymes that help break down your food. Like you, snakes have salivary glands. But over millions of years, the salivary glands of some species have evolved to make enzymes that are more and more toxic. In some snakes, those enzymes have become so deadly that they can paralyze nerves and stop blood from clotting!

PTUH!

Most snakes inject their venom into their victim when they bite. But some cobras have a backup weapon: They can also spit their venom from a distance! Spitting cobras are able to shoot jets of their venom from more than 6.5 feet (2 m) away. Although most snakes use venom to help them take down prey, spitting cobras use theirs for self-defense. They aim for their victims' eyes. If they land a hit, they can blind an attacker.

Mozambique spitting cobra

Lethal Lizards

Until recently, scientists thought that nearly all venomous reptiles were snakes. Only two species of venomous lizards were known: the Gila monster (p. 20) and the Mexican beaded lizard. But new research suggests that other lizards, such as iguanas and monitor lizards—which are often kept as pets—may make mild venom, too. Experts now think these lizards may share an ancestor with venomous snakes—one that lived about 200 million years ago.

Gila monster

To **REMEMBER THE DIFFERENCE BETWEEN POISONOUS AND VENOMOUS,** think of this: If an animal bites you and you get sick or die, it is venomous. If you bite an animal and you get sick or die, it's poisonous.

Venom vs. Poison

Venom and poison are not the same thing. Venomous reptiles such as cobras and Gila monsters deliver toxins with a nasty bite. Poisonous reptiles, in contrast, store toxins in their body tissues. These creatures are only toxic when eaten. That means there are very few truly poisonous reptiles—though there are a few. The green keelback snake, from South Asia, eats poisonous toads and keeps the poison in its skin. No human is known to have ever died from eating this snake—but it's possible!

Green keelback

SUN WORSHIPPERS

When the sun rises, reptiles emerge from their hiding places. They crawl, swim, and slither to rocks, floating logs, sidewalks—any spot where the sun shines. These scaly sunbathers warm their bodies using the sun's heat, a behavior called basking.

Ring-tailed dragon

Chill Out

All reptiles are ectothermic, more commonly known as cold-blooded. That means that their bodies can't usually create their own heat, like a human's does. Instead, they rely on heat from the sun to warm them. For this reason, most reptiles live in hot or warm places (remember, there are no reptiles in the Arctic or Antarctic). They bask by lying out in the sunshine to raise their body temperature. Reptiles most often bask in the morning. Once they've warmed up, they are able to take on other tasks, like searching for food or finding a mate.

Too Hot ... Too Cold ... Just Right!

By moving in and out of sunlight, reptiles can keep their bodies at a stable temperature. If they get too warm, reptiles retreat to a shady spot to keep from overheating. In the desert, where the temperature can climb dangerously high, most reptiles—along with most other desert creatures—stay in a cool spot such as an underground burrow during the hottest part of the day. They come out only at night, when things have cooled down.

Black iguana

Energy Savings

Moving in and out of sunny spots to warm your body might sound like a lot of work, but being cold-blooded has its advantages, too. Because a cold-blooded animal relies on the sun's energy to keep it warm, it doesn't have to use energy from its food for the task. That means that a reptile needs to spend less time hunting and eating than a similar-size mammal. That's one smart survival strategy!

Shovel-snouted lizard

The sands of the Namib desert in southern Africa, where the shovel-snouted lizard calls home, can reach a scorching 160°F (70°C)—hot enough to fry an egg! **TO KEEP FROM OVERHEATING, THE LIZARD STANDS ON JUST TWO OF ITS FEET AT A TIME, WHILE HOLDING UP THE OTHER TWO** so that they can cool off. Then it switches.

WORLD OF **REPTILES**

Reptiles live across most of planet Earth, from its oceans to its mountains to its deserts. In fact, this group of animals can be found in all types of habitats except polar ice and tundra. But where in the world do most of the 11,600 known species of reptiles make their homes?

Island Giants

Islands are home to some of Earth's largest reptiles, such as the Komodo dragon and the Galápagos tortoise. That's due to an effect called island gigantism. Sometimes, a species will get swept from the mainland to an island. There, it has no natural predators and can grow to enormous size.

Number of Reptile Species

- Greater than 75
- 26–75
- 1–25
- 0

Swimming Sea Snakes

Sea snakes inhabit warm regions of nearly every ocean. But there are no sea snakes in the Atlantic Ocean.

Color Code

In these maps, gray areas show where no species of reptiles live; green areas show where a few species live; and red areas show where many species live. In general, reptiles are clustered in warm places around the globe, such as rainforests and other tropical habitats. That makes sense for these heat-loving creatures.

North Pole

Alaska, U.S.A.

Iceland

Ireland

NORTH AMERICA

PACIFIC OCEAN

Galápagos Islands

SOUTH AMERICA

ATLANTIC OCEAN

AFR

SOUTHERN OCEAN

South Pole

ARCTIC OCEAN

Snake-Free Zones

Only a few places in the world have no snakes, including Ireland, Iceland, New Zealand, and some small islands in the Pacific. A few other areas are too cold for snakes: the northern-most parts of Russia and Europe; Alaska, U.S.A.; the southernmost tip of South America; and the two poles, of course.

R u s s i a

EUROPE

A S I A

I C A

PACIFIC OCEAN

INDIAN OCEAN

0   2,000 miles

0   2,000 kilometers

Lesser Sunda Islands

AUSTRALIA

New Zealand

Bad Rap

It's often said that Australia has the most dangerous snakes of any place in the world. But that's not really true! Although Australia does have the largest number of snakes that belong to the venomous snake family Elapidae, the group that includes cobras and black mambas, most Australian snakes in this family are very small or live under-ground, and are not dangerous to people.

A N T A R C T I C A

49

REPTILE BITES

Crocodiles and alligators **COOL DOWN BY OPENING THEIR MOUTHS** to release heat—similar to the way a dog pants.

Some reptiles **SWALLOW ROCKS** to help grind up their food.

You can't breathe when your mouth is full. **BUT A CROCODILE CAN,** by closing a valve at the back of its throat.

Some reptiles can **SEE COLOR BETTER THAN HUMANS CAN.**

Marine iguanas munch on **ALGAE AND SEAWEED.**

Most geckos can stick to almost any surface— **BUT NOT TEFLON,** the substance used to make nonstick pans.

Tortoises **ORBITED THE MOON** before astronauts did.

In some countries, like the United States and Australia, cows and other **LIVESTOCK CAUSE MORE HUMAN DEATHS** each year than venomous snakes do.

Saltwater crocodiles can live to be **75 YEARS OLD.**

Some monitor lizards like to bask in temperatures of **UP TO 150°F (66°C).** By contrast, a human's normal body temperature is about 98.6°F (37°C)!

LOVELY LIZARDS

>>> **THEY CAN HAVE HORNS, WINGS, OR FRILLS.** They can be nearly any color of the rainbow—or all the colors at once! They can be as small as a fingertip or nearly as long as a small car. They're the lizards. Here are some of the planet's most spectacular species.

Fan-Throated Lizard

A mottled brown male fan-throated lizard climbs atop a boulder on the dry plains of India. Arching his back, he stretches the front of his body upward until his nose is pointed at the sky and he is balanced on his front claws. Then he stretches out a flap of skin under his chin. This flap, called a fan, is covered in shimmering teal, blue, and orange scales. This eye-catching display is how the fan-throated lizard attracts a mate.

Web-Footed Gecko

This lizard is perfectly adapted for life in the reddish sands of Africa's Namib desert. Their webbed feet allow them to walk on top of the desert sand or bury themselves beneath it to stay cool during the scorching daylight hours. Their oversize eyes help them detect crickets and other prey at night, when they hunt. And their skin helps them blend in with their surroundings: These odd-looking lizards are almost see-through, with sandy-colored speckles.

Jackson's Chameleon

At first glance, it looks like a miniature triceratops. But it's actually a living creature called a Jackson's chameleon. Only male Jackson's chameleons have horns, which they use to defend their territory. Sometimes, two rival males will lock horns and try to shove each other off a tree branch. Jackson's chameleons live only in parts of Africa, but are often bred in captivity and kept as pets elsewhere.

Madagascar Giant Day Gecko

True to its name, the Madagascar giant day gecko can be a foot (30 cm) long. Despite its large size, this gecko is difficult to spot in the tropics of Madagascar, where its bright green coloring hides it against forest leaves. Although the most common sound reptiles make is a hiss, geckos can make a range of sounds from barks to croaks to squeaks. In fact, the name "gecko" likely came from the sound this lizard makes when clicking its wide tongue against the roof of its mouth.

Perentie

It's Australia's largest lizard, and the fourth largest lizard on Earth. Perenties use their forked tongues to sniff out prey, and they eat everything from birds to marsupials. And they aren't afraid to dine on venomous snakes, either! Once a perentie catches its prey, it will hold and shake it in its jaws until the animal dies. When threatened, perenties will scare off attackers by raising their huge bodies up and making a loud hissing sound.

STUPENDOUS SNAKES

>>> **SOME INJECT VENOM INTO THEIR PREY.** Others wrap their long bodies around and squeeze their prey to death. They're snakes, a group of close to 4,000 species that slither their way into almost every habitat on Earth.

Eyelash Palm Pit Viper

This snake is named for the pointed scales above its eyes, but that's not the first thing you'd probably notice: Its scales are often bright yellow, though this snake can also be green or pink. Eyelash palm pit vipers are some of the smallest venomous snakes in Central America, where they live in a range of forest habitats. This snake's rough scales may help protect it from poking branches and help it grip as it moves through the treetops.

White-Lipped Island Pit Viper

The color blue is incredibly rare in nature: Only a handful of animals on Earth are truly blue in color. That makes the brilliant blue hue of the white-lipped island pit viper from Komodo island of Indonesia all the more astonishing. This viper is as dangerous as it is beautiful. Although its venom rarely kills, a bite from one of these snakes is very painful, and it can cause swelling, severe bleeding, and tissue death.

San Francisco Garter Snake

It's sometimes called the most beautiful snake in North America. It's also one of the most endangered: The San Francisco garter snake lives only in coastal wetlands in San Mateo County, California, U.S.A. There, it feeds mainly on California red-legged frogs, which are also a threatened species. Though brilliant colors often signal that an animal is dangerous, garter snakes are gentle creatures.

Green Tree Python

When these snakes are adults, they turn the bright green color that gives them their name. But when they are born, they are bright yellow, orange, or red! Their coloring helps them blend into specific parts of their home range: the rainforests of New Guinea, eastern Indonesia, and northeastern Australia. Young red pythons, for example, are hard to spot among the decaying, reddish leaves on the forest floor.

Brazilian Rainbow Boa

When light passes through a prism, it is broken up into every color of the rainbow. That's what happens when light hits the skin of a rainbow boa. Tiny ridges on its scales act as prisms, turning the snake's skin shimmering colors. Why does the boa sport these rainbow hues? Scientists don't know yet!

Moment of AHA!!!

"I heard this high-pitched yelping sound coming from under my feet: the sound of baby crocodiles! They call out to let their brothers and sisters know that they're hatching, so that they can all emerge together, and to let their mother know, so that she can come dig them out. It was so late in the season that I knew something must have happened to this particular mother. If a nest is left too long, the babies won't make it because of scorching ground temperatures. So I dug out the eggs myself. I was the first thing this baby saw when it hatched!"

—Ru Somaweera

SHELLED AND SPECTACULAR

>>> **THEY CAN FIT IN THE PALM OF YOUR HAND OR BE AS HEAVY AS A GRAND PIANO.** They live in nearly every environment on Earth, from the ocean to some of the driest deserts. They're turtles, terrapins, and tortoises, and they include some of the most ancient species on the planet. Some have remained basically unchanged for hundreds of millions of years!

Yellow-Blotched Map Turtle

If you want to spot this turtle, visit the Pascagoula River in southern Mississippi, U.S.A. There, you might be lucky enough to see a yellow-blotched map turtle sunning itself on a fallen tree near the water. With its striped skin, yellow-spotted shell, and row of spines, this is one special species! The yellow-blotched map turtle's very small home range has experts concerned about its survival, and some zoos have begun breeding the turtles in captivity.

Pig-Nosed Turtle

Unlike any other turtle alive today, the pig-nosed turtle has a leathery shell, flippers like a sea turtle's, and of course, a long snout that looks like a pig's. It is the only surviving member of a family of turtles that have roamed the freshwaters of Australia since the time of the dinosaurs. Females lay their eggs in sandbars that dry up during summer. When the first rains of the wet season begin and nests flood, the eggs finally hatch.

Pancake Tortoise

It's not hard to guess where this tortoise got its name: It's as flat as a pancake! Unlike other members of its family, the pancake tortoise's flat shell is thin and flexible. As a result, the shell doesn't provide much protection from predators in its homeland of East Africa. Instead of relying on its shell to keep it safe, the pancake tortoise uses speed and flexibility. It is able to escape from predators quickly, and use the flexibility of its shell to hide in small cracks in rocks where other tortoises can't fit.

Radiated Tortoise

This tortoise with its striking shell is native to only one place in the world: a forest in the southern part of the island of Madagascar. Radiated tortoises are the largest of the "star" tortoises in the world, so called because of the starlike patterns on their shells. Unfortunately, this beautiful shell has put this tortoise at risk. Radiated tortoises are often taken from the wild to be sold as pets or to have their shells turned into decorative objects.

Cantor's Giant Softshell Turtle

A wide head and eyes positioned close to the mouth give this turtle its nickname: the frog-faced turtle. It's a softshell, a type of turtle with a squishy, leathery shell that includes some of the rarest species in the world. Cantor's giant softshell turtles, which make their home in Southeast Asia, can grow to the size of a small sofa and likely live more than 100 years. Like many other softshell turtles, they have been hunted for their meat nearly to extinction.

SNAKE **SENSES**

A snake may not look like it has a nose or ears. But just like you, it explores the world with smell and hearing—as well as sight, touch, and taste. In addition to these five basic senses, some species have a sixth sense: the ability to detect heat.

African bush viper

Sight

Some snakes that actively hunt their prey have a keen sense of sight. Scientists believe certain species may even have 3D vision. However, those that live underground or hunt at night do not—in fact, they can barely tell the difference between light and dark! Humans rely mostly on our eyes to sense the world around us, but snakes mainly use their senses of smell and touch.

Hearing

Humans hear when sound waves traveling through the air hit the eardrum and vibrate the tiny bones of the inner ear. Snakes don't have ears that you can see from outside, but they do have inner ears like ours. Vibrations traveling through the ground—such as the footsteps of their prey—vibrate their jawbones, which are connected to their inner ears.

Albino diamondback rattlesnake

Green tree python

Heat Sensors

Along with the five main senses, some snakes have a sixth sense: the ability to detect heat. Some pythons and boas have a row of small divots on their lip scales that are able to sense slight changes in the temperature around them. Because these snakes hunt small animals in the cool of night, this sense helps them detect prey. Some vipers have two supersensitive heat pits between their eyes and nostrils. In these snakes, the heat-detecting sense is so sophisticated that it sends an image to the snake's brain, allowing the snake to actually "see" in the dark using heat. That's one super sense!

Baird's rat snake scales

Smell

Snakes use their nostrils mostly for breathing. They do most of their smelling with their tongues! As a snake flicks its tongue in and out, it captures scent particles in the air and wafts them toward a special organ at the roof of its mouth called the Jacobson's organ, which detects smells.

Green rat snake

Touch

When you walk, only the bottoms of your feet are in contact with the ground. But when a snake slithers, its entire body touches the ground. A snake's long body is packed with sensors that can detect details like the size of nearby prey or which way a potential attacker is moving.

TOOTHY AND TERRIFIC

》》 MILLIONS OF YEARS AGO, WHEN DINOSAURS STOMPED ACROSS THE LANDSCAPE, ANOTHER KIND OF REPTILE MADE ITS HOME IN LAKES, RIVERS, AND SWAMPS: THE CROCODYLIANS. They were the perfect predators, with long jaws and sharp teeth—among the many traits that helped them survive climate shift, mass extinctions, and even the asteroid strike that killed most of their dinosaur relatives. They still lurk in Earth's waters today.

American Alligator

These giant animals, weighing as much as 1,000 pounds (454 kg), may seem like clumsy movers when they're on land. But in the water, they use webbed feet and a strong tail to swim fast and move with agility. In the mid-20th century, many people thought the American alligator was on the brink of extinction. These animals had been hunted until very few were left. But in 1967, a law prohibited hunting them. It worked: More than a million alligators roam the southeastern United States today.

Cuban Crocodile

Most crocodiles move slowly and heavily on land. Not Cuban crocodiles. These 10.5-foot (3.5-m) reptiles can move quickly and even leap in the air to snatch prey off low branches, thanks to powerful rear legs. These highly endangered crocodiles have the smallest range of any crocodile and now are found only in two swamps in Cuba.

Black Caiman

It's the largest predator in the Amazon, reaching up to 15 feet (4.6 m) from tail to snout. When black caimans are young and small, they eat mainly insects and crustaceans. But as they reach their adult size, they eat bigger prey, including fish and even the giant rodents called capybara. Their jaws are so strong that they can shatter turtle shells.

HOW DO YOU TELL AN ALLIGATOR FROM A CROCODILE? One way is by their teeth: A crocodile's fourth tooth in its lower jaw pokes out of its mouth when its jaw is closed. But an alligator's fourth lower tooth fits into a socket in its upper jaw and isn't visible.

Crocodile	Alligator
V-shaped snout	U-shaped snout
Visible lower teeth	Hidden lower teeth

Gharial

Gharials have much longer, narrower jaws than other crocodylians, with sharp, interlocking teeth that help the animal catch fish. Male gharials have a knobby growth at the end of their noses called the *ghara*. When the gharial calls, the ghara amplifies the sound into a loud buzzing noise that attracts females. One of the largest of all crocodylians, the gharial is so big that its legs aren't strong enough to carry its weight on land. Instead, it slides around on its belly. Gharials are critically endangered animals, with just a few hundred individuals left in the wild.

WHAT'S ON THE MENU?

If you've ever met a pet lizard, you know that their favorite foods include creepy-crawlies like mealworms and crickets. Many lizards are insectivores, a type of carnivore that gobbles up all kinds of insects, from beetles to bees. But not all reptiles survive this way. Here are a few with truly unique tastes.

Tiny to Mighty

Although most reptiles are carnivores, their prey can range in size from very small to very big. The tiny nano chameleon (p. 156) munches on mites. African rock pythons, on the other hand, have been known to swallow impalas whole. That's what you call a big meal!

Tree for Me

With their tree-living lifestyle, lizards called anoles live in the perfect location to snag their preferred prey: insects. Anoles love to snack on crickets, flies, and spiders. But some have a taste for a totally different kind of food. Scientists have observed wild anoles lapping up tree sap! Whether they do it for nourishment or because they're thirsty is a mystery.

Salad Bar

Some reptiles prefer a vegetarian diet. Although many reptiles will occasionally snack on plants, tortoises and some iguanas eat nothing else. Their bodies are specially adapted to survive on a diet of vines, leaves, grasses, flowers, and fruits. Galápagos tortoises especially love to eat prickly pear cactus!

Bugging Out

Blind snakes (also called worm snakes) live underground, slithering their wormlike bodies through the soft soil and tunnels left behind by termites and ants. While they're at it, they munch on the animals that built these burrows, and also their eggs and larvae. That's no way to repay a host!

Fish Dinner

Humans will pay thousands of dollars for a single ounce of caviar, the eggs of a certain type of fish called sturgeon. But sea snakes dine on fish eggs for free. A few species, such as turtle-headed sea snakes, eat nothing else. They don't have teeth like other sea snakes do—instead, they have very tough bony plates and lips to help them scrape off fish eggs from rocks and corals. How fancy!

Shelled Supper

The African egg-eating snake survives by eating one food and one food only: birds' eggs! Thanks to its highly flexible jaws, it can swallow eggs—which can be several times larger than its head—whole! Sharp spikes at the back of its throat pierce the shells. Then the snake swallows the contents and coughs up empty shells.

FACE-TO-FACE

WITH A
FRILLED LIZARD

WHEN YOU TALK ABOUT THE WORLD'S MOST ICONIC REPTILES, THE FRILLED-NECK LIZARD IS RIGHT AT THE TOP. Growing up as a reptile lover, I had always wanted to see one, but none of the zoos I visited as a kid had them. When I first came to Australia in 2007, I went directly to the Northern Territory—the remote Australian outback. I was excited, because I was there to help with a project dedicated to understanding more about frilled lizards, or frillies, as they're nicknamed. This is a photo from my first day, and the first frilly I ever saw.

Unlike most reptiles that take cover when the sun is at its hottest, frillies are most active around the middle of the day under the baking sun. They spend most of their time in trees, but they come down during this time to eat ants, termites, and other insects. For this project, we had to catch them using a long noose, a loop of rope that you get around their necks. We caught this one while it was resting on a tree trunk.

For this study, we collected all kinds of data from the frillies we caught. We took measurements, checked for parasites and injuries, and put microchips in them. Later in the year, we went back and caught them again. We were able to scan the microchips to find out which lizard we had caught, and then we could see how much they had grown and changed. It's not easy to do this, because these animals are fierce! They have long, pointy teeth and big heads, so if you are bitten, they can do serious damage.

The frilled-neck lizard is a fascinating species. It's the only one in its group (called a genus), meaning there is nothing else like it on Earth. It resembles a dinosaur from the prehistoric! We think they use the frill for defense and as a threat display to intimidate rivals. But there are many other theories. It could be for attracting females, or it could help the frilly keep cool—the same way an elephant's ears help cool the animal by running its blood close to the air. There are even some old—and almost certainly wrong—ideas, like they use the frill to parachute from treetops! But nobody is totally sure. It's one of the mysteries we hope to solve by studying this unusual species.

Draco lizard

CHAPTER THREE

AMAZING ADAPTATIONS

>>> IT'S NOT EASY TO SURVIVE 300 MILLION YEARS ON EARTH. To eat and keep from being eaten, generation after generation, reptiles have had to develop some savvy survival skills. Some shed body parts on purpose to escape the clutches of an attacker. Others become airborne as they move from tree to tree in their forest home.

These abilities are called adaptations—traits that help living things survive. And reptiles are known for having some of the most incredible adaptations in the animal kingdom.

PANTHER CHAMELEON

WHERE IT'S FOUND:
Madagascar

FUN FACT: A second layer of crystals in the chameleon's skin reflects away sunlight—like built-in sunscreen.

>>> **WHEN TWO MALE PANTHER CHAMELEONS MEET IN THE WILD, THEY PUT ON QUITE A SHOW.** In an effort to intimidate its rival, one chameleon turns the yellow hue of a highlighter, while the other shifts to a bright cherry red. Whichever chameleon loses this battle of the boldest will turn tail and leave. Male panther chameleons also display their brightest colors in the hopes of wooing a female. And if she's not interested, she'll let him know—by using her own color-changing ability to shift to a darker hue.

For a long time, scientists weren't sure how chameleons pulled off their incredible color displays. But recently, they learned that these animals have microscopic crystals in their skin. When a chameleon gets excited, its crystal pattern shifts, changing the way light bounces off its skin.

NO TAIL, NO PROBLEM

Out of the air, a hawk takes a sudden dive. It's aiming for a lizard sunning itself on a rock. The hawk grasps with its clawed feet and manages to grab hold of the lizard's wriggling tail. But that's all it is—just a tail. The lizard has detached its tail to distract its attacker! Meanwhile, the lizard has scurried off to safety.

Dtella gecko

Losing It

Like you, a lizard has a line of small bones, called vertebrae, that runs down its back. In lizards, the vertebrae continue into a long tail. But the tails of some lizards have several weak points called fracture planes. If the lizard is in a life-or-death situation, muscles along these planes pull apart, causing the tail to fall off at one of the weak points.

When a lizard drops its tail, the tail's nerves continue to work. That makes the tail thrash and wiggle on the ground. Sometimes, a detached tail can keep moving for about half an hour. That keeps the predator distracted, giving the lizard enough time to escape.

Ctenotus skink

Sometimes when a lizard **LOSES ITS TAIL, ITS BODY WILL REGROW MORE THAN ONE.** In one incident, an Argentine black-and-white tegu was documented sprouting six tails!

Growth Spurt

After it drops its tail, the lizard has another trick to perform: It regrows the lost body part. The replacement tail is usually not quite the same as the old one: It's often made of cartilage, the bendy substance that makes up your ears and the tip of your nose. And it can take a lizard months to regrow a tail. Some species of lizards can't regrow them at all.

Scientists are hard at work studying this ability, called regeneration. If they can figure out how lizards are able to regrow their tails, they might be able to grow new arms and legs for humans who have lost a limb.

REPTILES THAT SOAR

>>> **SOMETHING WHIPS BETWEEN THE TREES, HIGH ABOVE THE GROUND.** It's not a bird or a bat. It's a reptile! Many snakes and lizards live in trees. To move around the forest, they have to travel across the ground, which takes up valuable time and energy, and makes them vulnerable to predators. So a few species have evolved a nifty way to move from tree to tree without ever touching the ground.

Draco Lizard

When it wants to zip to a new tree, the Draco lizard extends a set of extra-long ribs, unfurling folds of skin. It leaps from its tree, using its skin flaps like a parachute to catch the wind and glide. This lizard can zoom as far as 30 feet (9 m), steering with its long, thin tail. Male Dracos use their gliding ability to guard their territories. They soar between two or three trees that they have claimed as their own to chase off rivals.

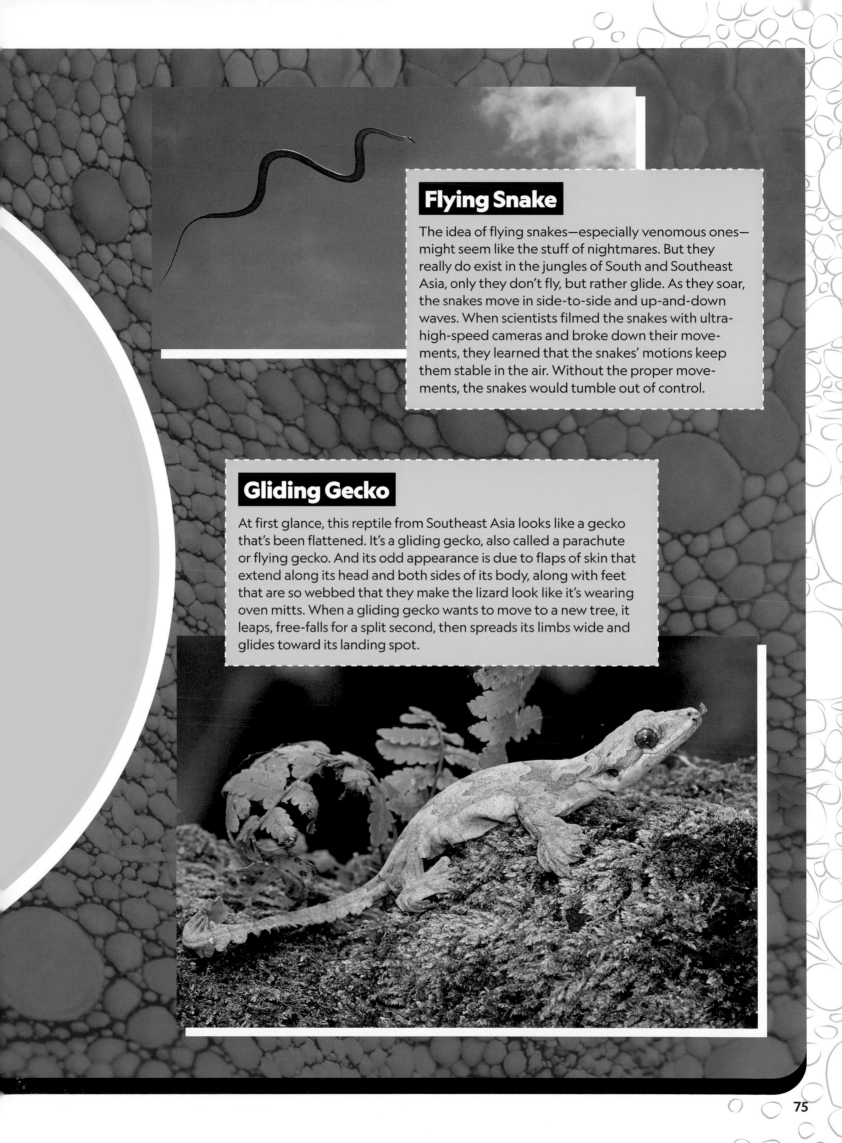

Flying Snake

The idea of flying snakes—especially venomous ones—might seem like the stuff of nightmares. But they really do exist in the jungles of South and Southeast Asia, only they don't fly, but rather glide. As they soar, the snakes move in side-to-side and up-and-down waves. When scientists filmed the snakes with ultra-high-speed cameras and broke down their movements, they learned that the snakes' motions keep them stable in the air. Without the proper movements, the snakes would tumble out of control.

Gliding Gecko

At first glance, this reptile from Southeast Asia looks like a gecko that's been flattened. It's a gliding gecko, also called a parachute or flying gecko. And its odd appearance is due to flaps of skin that extend along its head and both sides of its body, along with feet that are so webbed that they make the lizard look like it's wearing oven mitts. When a gliding gecko wants to move to a new tree, it leaps, free-falls for a split second, then spreads its limbs wide and glides toward its landing spot.

"In Australia, the green tree python is only found in very few rainforests. It does something very unusual: It completely changes its color when it reaches adulthood. Babies are born bright red or yellow and turn green when they are between six and 12 months old. This drastic color change happens quite fast—in about a week or two. So finding one like this that was in the middle of changing color is really exciting."

—Ru Somaweera

REPTILE BITES

The group of eggs a turtle lays is **CALLED A CLUTCH.**

Several species of small lizards called anoles can stay underwater for at least 16 minutes at a time by **BREATHING FROM A BUBBLE OF AIR** that they bring along with them—similar to a scuba diver's tank!

Sea snakes are **RELATED TO COBRAS.**

A turtle's **TOP SHELL IS CALLED A CARAPACE.** Its bottom shell is called a plastron.

Green sea turtles get their **NAME FROM THE COLOR OF THEIR FAT,** which is green because of the turtle's diet of seagrasses and algae.

Vipers have **HINGED FANGS THAT FOLD UP** when not in use.

Hawksbill turtles use their pointed, narrow beaks to pluck their favorite food— **SEA SPONGES—** from coral reefs.

Chameleons can **MOVE EACH EYE INDEPENDENTLY** of the other.

Some snakes use folds of skin in their lower jaw to **SOAK UP WATER,** like a sponge.

SNAKES DON'T BLINK because they don't have eyelids.

COOLEST COPYCATS

>>> STARE AS HARD AS YOU CAN INTO THE FOREST WHERE THESE REPTILES LURK, AND YOU PROBABLY WON'T SPOT THEM. That's because these snakes and lizards don't look like snakes and lizards at all. Over millions of years of evolution, their bodies have altered to mimic the environment around them.

Satanic Leaf-Tailed Gecko

When this lizard feels threatened, it stares directly at its foe, opens its mouth wide to show the bright red inside, and cries out loudly. This behavior may look a bit devilish—and it's one of the traits that inspired the creature's name. But most of the time, the satanic leaf-tailed gecko rests motionless on the forest floor or hangs limply from a branch. There, it manages to look exactly like a dead leaf. It mimics every detail, with lines on its skin that look just like a leaf's veins, greenish spots that resemble moss, and even pieces missing from its tail, like a rotting leaf.

Mata Mata

With its rows of spikes, it looks like an armored dinosaur. But the mata is actually a freshwater turtle that lives in South America. Its bumpy shell, head, and neck make it look like a pile of rotting leaves at the bottom of the tropical rivers where this turtle dwells. When a fish gets too close, the mata will open its jaws, creating a vacuum with its mouth and—*whoosh!*—suck in its meal.

Green Vine Snake

These snakes live on bushes and trees in Asia. With their green scales and thin bodies the width of a human finger, they look just like the vines they're named after. To make the disguise even more convincing, green vine snakes often gently sway their bodies to look like foliage moving in the breeze. The snakes even flick their tongues at very slow speed, so the motion doesn't give them away. When they smell prey nearby, they move toward it slowly until they get close enough to strike. Then they release venom from fangs located at the back of their jaws to paralyze their victim for easy eating.

Pebble-Mimic Dragon

These lizards live in an odd habitat: open and stony plains in the western part of Australia covered in small, bright white rocks called quartz. Most creatures would stand out in this landscape. But not the pebble-mimic dragon. This animal's bulbous body and pale brown and white colors make it look like just another clump of pebbles. When it's not scuttling around, pebble-mimic dragons stand perfectly still with their legs tucked in, making them nearly impossible to spot.

SHOCKING SURVIVAL

You've heard of venomous snakes and lizards with convincing camouflage. But these animals take staying alive to the next level. Meet some reptiles with truly unusual adaptations.

Super Slumber

You might know that when winter comes, bears clamber into their dens and enter a sleeplike state until spring arrives. But did you know that crocodylians do the same thing? When conditions get too hot or too cold, some will dig a burrow into a riverbank and snuggle up tight. For example, the Chinese alligator, the closest relative of the American alligator, can spend more than half the year brumating inside large tunnels that they dig. Brumating is a state similar to hibernating, and it helps crocodylians survive during harsh times with little food.

Sipping Water From Sand

It might sound like a magic trick. But the thorny devil has evolved a clever way to drink in Australia's driest deserts: It can use its skin like a straw. When it gets thirsty, the lizard moves on to wet soil or sand patches. Tiny channels between its scales pull moisture out of the sand and along its body to its mouth. Then the lizard gulps down the water.

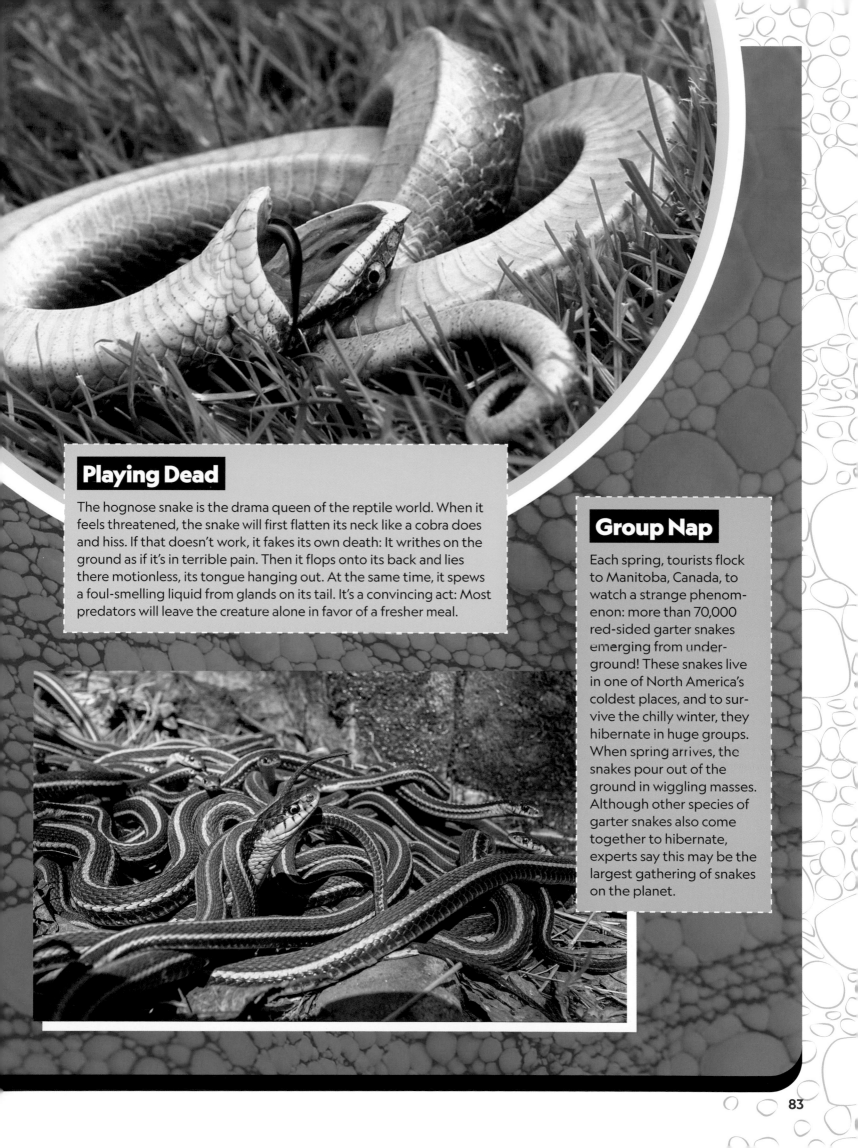

Playing Dead

The hognose snake is the drama queen of the reptile world. When it feels threatened, the snake will first flatten its neck like a cobra does and hiss. If that doesn't work, it fakes its own death: It writhes on the ground as if it's in terrible pain. Then it flops onto its back and lies there motionless, its tongue hanging out. At the same time, it spews a foul-smelling liquid from glands on its tail. It's a convincing act: Most predators will leave the creature alone in favor of a fresher meal.

Group Nap

Each spring, tourists flock to Manitoba, Canada, to watch a strange phenomenon: more than 70,000 red-sided garter snakes emerging from underground! These snakes live in one of North America's coldest places, and to survive the chilly winter, they hibernate in huge groups. When spring arrives, the snakes pour out of the ground in wiggling masses. Although other species of garter snakes also come together to hibernate, experts say this may be the largest gathering of snakes on the planet.

GREEN BASILISK LIZARD

>>> **THE GREEN BASILISK LIZARD SPENDS MOST OF ITS TIME IN TREES.** But it makes sure to never stray far from a body of water. That's because, if threatened, this lizard can deploy one of the most unusual tricks in the animal kingdom: It drops from its tree into the water—and sprints away across the surface! To pull off this trick, the basilisk lizard uses fringes of skin between its long rear toes that unfurl when it steps onto the water. As it runs, it slaps its feet hard against the water's surface, trapping a bubble of air under its toes that keeps the lizard from sinking. As long as it moves fast, it can cover 15 feet (4.6 m) or more this way. This unusual habit of "walking on water" has given the lizard its nickname: the Jesus Christ lizard.

 WHERE IT'S FOUND: Rainforests of Central America

 FUN FACT: Green basilisk lizards can run on water.

ON THE MOVE

Reptiles slither, crawl, and glide. But a few species are known for much more unusual ways of getting around—or away. Meet some of the more unique reptile movers on the planet.

Bite Me

The armadillo girdled lizard has impressive armor: Rows of spiny scales cover its body, head, and tail. But the lizard has one vulnerable part: its soft belly. So when it senses danger, the armadillo girdled lizard will roll up into a ball and bite its own tail, protecting its underside and exposing its spikes to predators while sometimes rolling away. No wonder it's named after the armadillo, a mammal known for the same behavior.

Swimming Through Sand

When the sun sinks below the horizon in the American West, the western shovel-nosed snake pokes its head out of the ground. Once it senses that the coast is clear, it slithers out and away, on the hunt for insects, spiders, and scorpions. The snake has a long, flat nose, and just like the garden tool it's named after, it is excellent at digging into the ground. This, along with its smooth scales, allows the snake to wiggle right through sandy desert soil.

Galloping Gait

Horses are known for their fast, bounding gait. But only a handful of reptiles are known to move this way. One is the Australian freshwater crocodile. When startled, this animal can spring into a gallop, holding its belly and tail off the ground as it runs away from danger. It is believed that this not only makes for a faster escape but also helps to avoid bumping into obstacles such as rocks and logs on banks. Crocodiles have been clocked galloping at speeds of 11 miles an hour (18 km/h).

Slithering Sideways

If you've ever visited a beach, you know that walking across sand isn't easy. That's because it shifts underfoot, making the trek slow going. Snakes living in sandy places face the same challenge. That's why sidewinders—a group that includes snakes in the deserts of Africa, the Middle East, and North America—move by slithering sideways, not forward. Most snake species have microscopic spikes on their undersides that dig into the ground as they move forward. Sidewinders, in contrast, sport tiny pits on their bellies that grip the ground no matter which direction the snake is moving. That adaptation helps the sidewinding rattlesnake move at up to 18 miles an hour (29 km/h).

FACE-TO-FACE

WITH A SANDSTONE LONG-NECKED TURTLE

EVERY YEAR, I GO OUT WITH MY TEAM TO THREE DIFFERENT RIVERS IN THE REMOTE AUSTRALIAN OUT-BACK TO NET CROCODILES. We go during the dry season, when the rivers have dried up until they are just pools of water. That's the best time because then every animal that lives in that river system, from fish to crocodiles, is forced to be in those pools. We've even found bull sharks there, 180 miles (300 km) from the ocean! We lay nets across the pools and startle the animals so that they swim into the nets. That gives us a way to study all the crocodiles that live there and track how they are doing from year to year. After we take measurements, we let them go until the next year.

On this particular trip, we were shocked to find this giant thing in one of our nets.

It's called a sandstone long-necked turtle. And what's amazing about it is its size. Australia doesn't have giant turtles the way that some other places, including the United States, do. The average shell length of an Australian turtle is about seven inches (18 cm). But this thing had a shell double that, at 14 inches (36 cm), and a total length of about 28 inches (70 cm). As turtles go, that's not enormous. But no turtle of this species close to that size had been discovered in Australia—until we caught this one!

That experience showed me that some of the most amazing discoveries happen by accident. The turtle was not the target of our research. Unlike humans, reptiles keep growing as long as they live. Once a turtle gets that large, nothing can eat it, but there is a lot that it can eat. So this particular turtle probably found a place with a supply of good food, and it just kept growing and growing.

Catching this big turtle also showed that our knowledge often comes from very limited observations. It could be that many big turtles are living in Australia, but we just haven't discovered them yet. Sometimes total chance encounters like this one expand our scientific knowledge.

Komodo dragon

CHAPTER FOUR

DEADLY HUNTERS

>>> THEY LURK UNDERWATER, JUST THEIR EYES AND NOSES ABOVE THE SURFACE TO SENSE ANY SIGNS OF NEARBY PREY. They dangle from tree limbs, waiting for a hapless victim to wander underneath. They hide in underground burrows, biding their time until the dark of night, when they can crawl out and sniff the air for their next meal.

Some of the planet's most skilled hunters are reptiles. Some stalk their prey, often using camouflage to blend in with the background while they slowly inch close enough to strike. Others are ambush predators. They sit motionless, waiting for a tasty critter to venture close enough to catch. Then … *CHOMP!* Flip the page to meet some of the deadliest hunters ever.

BOA CONSTRICTOR

>>> **A BOA CONSTRICTOR SNOOZES IN A HOLLOW LOG.** Normally, this snake's body is long and lean. But right now, its middle is stretched around an enormous lump. That lump is a dead wild pig that the snake swallowed the day before. Now, while the snake rests, its strong stomach acids digest the food.

After a big meal, boa constrictors don't eat again for weeks. When they do get hungry, they will lie in wait for prey to wander close. Boa constrictors can be tan, green, red, or yellow and come in many different patterns to suit the environment they need to blend into. Boas can grow up to 13 feet (4 m) long and weigh more than a 13-year-old kid. They ambush and wrap their bodies around prey such as rats, monkeys, or pigs until it suffocates. Then they swallow their victims whole.

WHERE IT'S FOUND: Tropics of Central and South America

FUN FACT: Boa constrictors don't lay eggs. Instead, they give birth to as many as 60 live babies at a time.

KOMODO DRAGON

>>> THE KOMODO DRAGON IS THE LARGEST LIVING LIZARD IN THE WORLD, GROWING UP TO 10 FEET (3 M) LONG AND WEIGHING NEARLY 200 POUNDS (90 KG) IN THE WILD, AS MUCH AS A FULL-GROWN HUMAN. It's not just their huge size that gives them the name "dragon"—these reptiles also have a long, forked yellow tongue. When the mega-lizard flicks its tongue in the air, it looks a bit like a mythical dragon spitting fire!

Most of the time, Komodo dragons survive by eating small animals and carrion, or dead animals. But occasionally, they will attack large animals such as deer and water buffalo. They hunt this big prey by lying in ambush in long grass. When their intended victim passes by, a Komodo dragon will use its sharp teeth and claws to attack, killing most victims immediately. But even if the prey manages to escape, it's usually too late: A single bite from a Komodo dragon is a death sentence. Their venomous saliva contains chemicals that stop blood from clotting, causing their victims to bleed to death. As if that weren't enough, the mouth of a Komodo dragon also contains some 60 different strains of bacteria that cause deadly infection. All the Komodo dragon has to do is take its time following until its prey is too weak to fight back or dies—and then it's mealtime. *Yikes!*

94

FUN FACT: A Komodo dragon can eat more than five pounds (2.3 kg) of meat—the equivalent of 20 hamburger patties—per minute.

GONE FISHING

>>> **TO FIND PREY, SOME PREDATORS DON'T NEED TO GO HUNTING.** These snakes prefer a more laid-back approach: They use specially modified tails to attract their next meal, just like fishermen use bait.

Spider-Tailed Horned Viper

A bird swoops to snap up a tasty spider. But instead of getting a meal, it *becomes* a meal. What looks like a spider is actually a growth at the end of a strange snake's tail. The spider-tailed horned viper's brown-and-white coloration perfectly camouflages its body against its rocky habitat. The only thing that stands out is the end of its bulb-shaped tail, which is covered in long, thin scales that resemble spider legs. The snake is an expert at jiggling this bait to mimic the movements of a spider. What bird could resist?

Dusky Pygmy Rattlesnake

Some people think a rattlesnake's rattle is similar to a maraca, with bits inside that clatter around. But a rattle is actually formed of multiple segments made of keratin, the substance your fingernails are made of. These segments fit loosely together, so that when the snake shakes its tail tip, they make a noise. Rattlesnakes use their rattle to scare off attackers. But scientists believe that the ancestors of rattlesnakes may have instead used their rattles to lure prey close. One species, the dusky pygmy rattlesnake, still does this. Its rattle sounds like the buzzing of an insect.

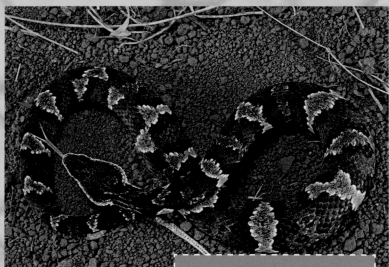

Taylor's Cantil

As adults, Taylor's cantils use a pair of elaborate fangs to take down prey. The fangs are hinged, and most of the time they lie flat in the snake's mouth. But when the cantil strikes, its fangs swing forward into position to drive deep into the prey's tissue. Adult Taylor's cantils use a quick strike to capture prey. But young cantils have an additional trick: a brightly colored lure at the end of their tails that the snakes wiggle as bait. When the snakes reach adulthood, the lure disappears.

Death Adder

With its short, wide body, the death adder doesn't exactly look like one of the fastest-striking snakes on the planet. But it is. This creature, native to Australia, New Guinea, and Indonesia, spends most of its time lying completely motionless, blending into its surroundings. The only thing moving is the tip of the snake's tail, which looks like a worm. The snake twitches its tail tip to attract skinks, its favorite prey. When a skink comes close, the death adder deploys the deadly venom that gives this snake its name.

>>> A CHAMELEON'S STICKY TONGUE IS A HIGH-SPEED WEAPON. Coils of muscles launch the tongue outward. The tongue's tip is coated with mucus so sticky it can hold prey weighing one-third of the chameleon's body weight. It ensnares a tasty insect, then a second set of muscles reels the tongue back in, along with the captured prey. *Gulp!*

Surprisingly, some of the smaller chameleons have the most powerful tongues. The rosette-nosed chameleon, a tiny reptile about the size of a human thumb, can extend its tongue out more than twice the length of its body and—at 8,500 feet per second (2,600 m/s)—faster than the fastest sports car!

ROSETTE-NOSED CHAMELEON

WHERE IT'S FOUND:
Tanzania, Africa

FUN FACT: A space shuttle accelerates at up to three times the force of gravity. This chameleon's tongue accelerates at up to 264 times the force of gravity.

OLIVE SEA SNAKE

>>> **IT BREATHES AIR, JUST LIKE ALL LAND-DWELLING SNAKES.** But the olive sea snake—like all other sea snakes—spends its entire life in the ocean. Many special adaptations help this reptile survive a life at sea: Thanks to a lung that extends almost the length of the body, it can go for hours between breaths at the surface. It has a flattened tail that works like a paddle to help it swim. It even has light-sensing organs in its tail that help it hide in a dark crevice during the day.

This ocean dweller is one of the largest sea snake species on Earth, reaching lengths of more than five feet (1.5 m). It lives mainly in coral reefs, where it hunts fish and shellfish. It paralyzes its victims with extremely toxic venom. Though the venom is lethal enough to kill a human, olive sea snakes will not attack unless a person tries to grab them.

WHERE IT'S FOUND:
Warm waters in the Indo-Pacific

FUN FACT: Olive sea snakes aren't aggressive, but they will sometimes follow snorkelers and scuba divers out of curiosity.

REPTILE BITES

ALL TORTOISES ARE TURTLES, but not all turtles are tortoises.

A human's heart has four chambers—and so do the hearts of all crocodylians. But all other reptiles have a **THREE-CHAMBERED HEART.**

Many reptiles eat their prey **WHOLE.**

Most geckos **DON'T HAVE EYELIDS.** They lick their eyeballs to clean them.

In 2020, a *Tyrannosaurus rex* fossil sold for **MORE THAN $31 MILLION.**

The top Jurassic predator was a **GIANT CROCODILE** about as long as an African elephant.

Crocodiles sometimes **SHED TEARS WHILE THEY'RE EATING.** Experts aren't yet sure why.

Spitting cobras can **SPRAY JETS OF VENOM** into an attacker's eyes.

A group of rattlesnakes is **CALLED A RHUMBA.**

Turtles and tortoises can **FEEL A TOUCH TO THEIR SHELLS.**

ALLIGATOR SNAPPING TURTLE

>>> **SOME SAY IT LOOKS MORE LIKE A DINOSAUR THAN A TURTLE.** And with its spiky shell and beak-like mouth, the alligator snapping turtle does appear to be something from a prehistoric era. It inhabits the rivers, lakes, and canals of the southeastern United States, where it spends nearly its entire life in the water. It's the largest freshwater turtle in North America, with some males on record weighing in at more than 220 pounds (100 kg).

The alligator snapping turtle depends on its fishing ability to survive. It hunts by lying on the river bottom and opening its jaws wide to display a bright red, wormlike appendage on its tongue. When a curious fish swims close to investigate, the turtle lives up to its name: *SNAP!*

WHERE IT'S FOUND:
Central and southeastern United States

(i) **FUN FACT:** Because of their protective body armor and large size, adult snapping turtles have no natural predators.

"Some animals have no color pigment in their skin. Their eyes are even pink, because you can see the blood inside them! This is a genetic mutation called albinism. It's not unusual for babies to be born this way. But since albino animals are very visible to predators, they rarely survive to adulthood. That made spotting this fully grown albino cobra incredibly cool."

—Ru Somaweera

Moment of AHA!!!

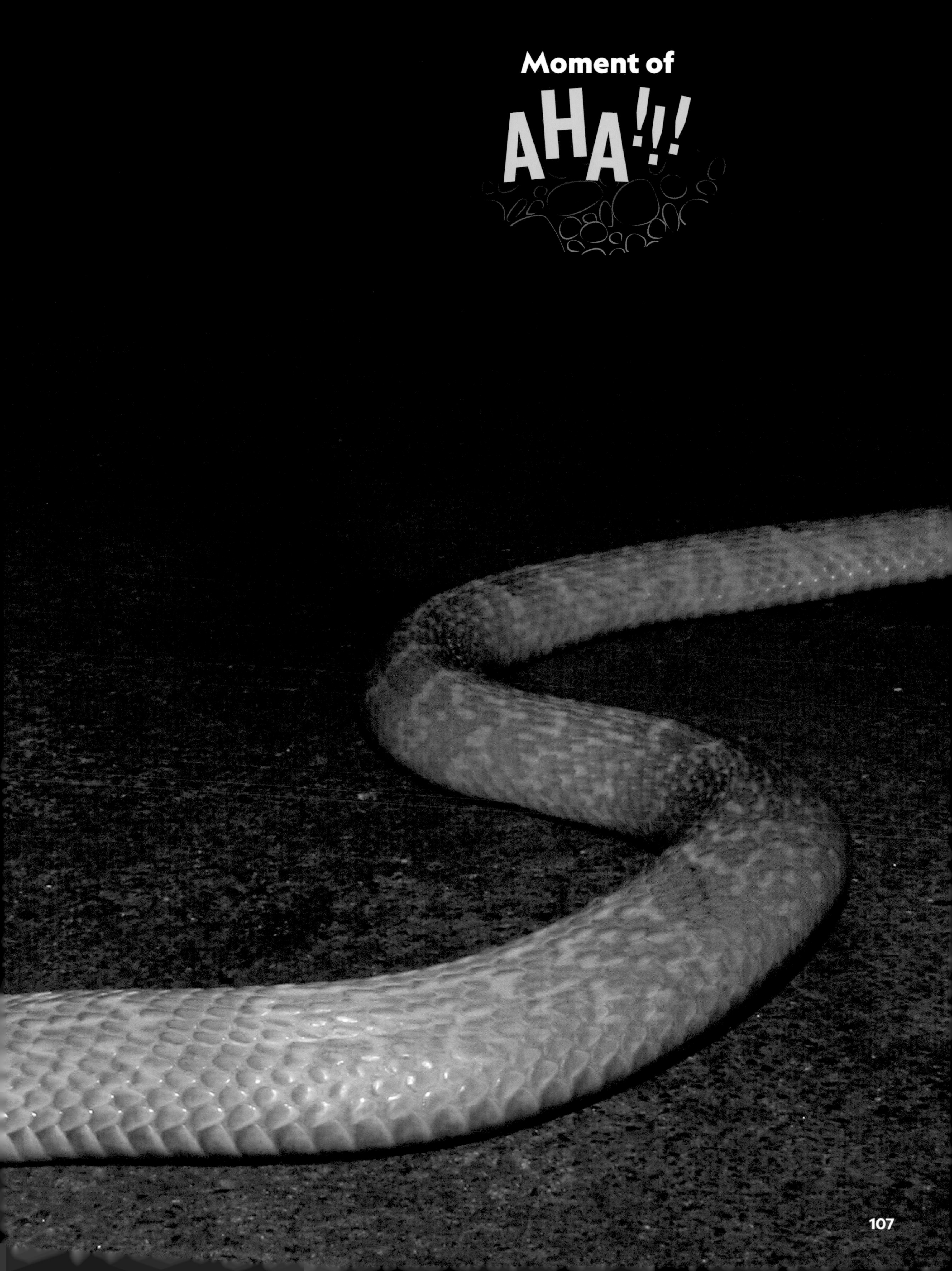

YELLOW-RED RAT SNAKE

>>> EVERY NIGHT, COUNTLESS BATS ZIP THROUGH THE AIR, GOBBLING UP INSECTS ABOVE LAKE CHICHANCANAB, NEAR THE TOWN OF KANTEMÓ, MEXICO. But when the bats return to their cave at the end of the night, they have to face a lethal obstacle course: Snakes dangle from the cave's ceiling, waiting to grab the bats out of the air as they enter and leave the cave. Their lair is called the Cave of the Hanging Serpents.

These yellow-red rat snakes can't see well in the dark or hear. But they are formidable predators all the same. They can sense the vibrations of bats flying by in total darkness, and when they do, they strike with deadly accuracy. Once a snake captures a bat, it pulls its prey inside a crevice in the cave's ceiling to dine in peace.

WHERE IT'S FOUND: Cave systems and rocky areas in Mexico's Yucatan Peninsula

FUN FACT: One cave where this snake is found is home to other strange creatures, including a transparent eel.

FIGHTING BACK

When these reptiles are cornered, they don't back down: They fight back. But they don't just bite or hiss. These species have developed some of the reptile kingdom's most unusual defenses.

Blue-Tongued Skink

When this lizard wants to intimidate a rival, it puffs up its body and sticks out its tongue. That might not sound all that alarming. But just like its name indicates, this creature's tongue is bright blue! The color is a warning to would-be attackers that the skink may be toxic to eat. The flash of color is often enough to surprise potential predators, buying the skink precious time so that it can scurry away.

Toadhead Agama

The toadhead agama looks like a normal desert-dwelling lizard ... that is, until it gets upset. Then it turns on its foe, curls its tail up over its back like a scorpion, hisses, and unfurls flaps on the sides of its mouth. The flaps are pink in color, and when they are spread wide, they make the lizard look like it's got the mouth of a much bigger and more ferocious creature. This display is enough to make almost any attacker back down!

Toothy Transport

A female crocodile buries her eggs in a mound or underground nest and spends months guarding them from predators. When the baby crocodiles are ready to hatch, they start to chirp from within the nest. When she hears their cries, the mother digs down into the nest to free her little ones. Then she tenderly picks up her babies in her massive jaws and carries them to the water. It was once thought that crocodile fathers didn't participate. But scientists now know that some daddy crocs will help transport their young to the water, too.

Sitting Pretty

Most snakes lay their eggs and then slither away, leaving their little ones' survival up to fate. But not king cobras. They are the only snakes in the world that are known to build and guard a nest. The female cobra will drag leaves and small sticks into a pile that can be two feet (0.6 m) high and six feet (1.8 m) across. Then she'll lay up to 40 eggs inside and cover them up. Cobras don't incubate their eggs with their bodies to keep them warm like birds do—instead, the mother cobra relies on heat produced by the rotting leaves that form her nest. But she does coil up on top of the pile, ready to strike at any predators looking for an eggy snack.

A CASE OF MISTAKEN IDENTITY

Only about one in five snake species have some form of venom system. But some nonvenomous snakes have evolved a sneaky strategy: They mimic the colors and patterns of deadlier snakes. These copycats may look dangerous—but it's all an act!

King Snake vs. Coral Snake

"Red touch yellow, kill a fellow." That rhyme helps hikers in parts of the southern United States identify the coral snake, the United States' most toxic snake. The coral snake isn't hard to spot. In fact, its black, red, and yellow stripes are there to make it stand out, serving as a warning to would-be attackers. That's what makes a copycat pattern such a great disguise for the nonvenomous king snake. It's good enough to fool many humans, but it isn't perfect: The king snake's yellow stripes are sandwiched by black ones, while the real deal has bands of yellow that separate its red and black stripes.

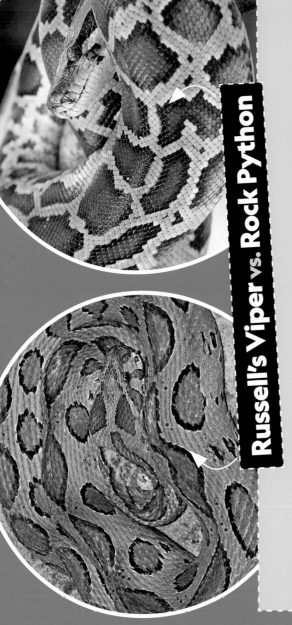

Russell's Viper vs. Rock Python

Enormous in size at up to 16 feet (5 m), with a beautiful pattern of golden and brown patches, the Indian rock python is commonly found in farmlands and is often encountered by farmers working in the field. This snake isn't venomous—like other pythons, it kills its prey by squeezing it to death. But farmers had still better be careful: The Russell's viper, which is quite similar in color to small pythons and is also common in farmlands, is one of the most venomous snakes in all of South Asia. Its bite can cause severe swelling, bleeding, organ failure, and often death.

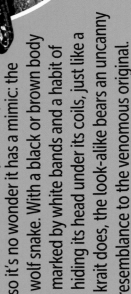

Common Krait vs. Wolf Snake

Many people fear the common krait, and with good reason: A bite from a krait is often painless, but it's highly venomous. As the venom sets in, the victim's muscles become paralyzed, and death follows shortly behind. It's a snake most creatures want to stay far away from—so it's no wonder it has a mimic: the wolf snake. With a black or brown body marked by white bands and a habit of hiding its head under its coils, just like a krait does, the look-alike bears an uncanny resemblance to the venomous original.

Indian Cobra vs. Indian Rat Snake

The cobra is one of the most characteristic snakes out there. When a cobra feels threatened, it raises the front of its body off the ground and unfurls its hood to appear larger and more menacing. Though the Indian rat snake lacks a true hood, it will rise up and inflate its neck, looking enough like a cobra to send many a panicked human running. But although a cobra's bite can be dangerous, a rat snake's is entirely harmless to humans (although it probably wouldn't feel good!).

FACE-TO-FACE

WITH KOMODO DRAGONS

OF ALL THE ADVENTURES THAT I HAVE HAD IN MY LIFE WHEN IT COMES TO REPTILES, THIS WAS THE MOST MEMORABLE: FINDING KOMODO DRAGONS. It took years of planning and saving up. But finally, in 2016, I took my first trip. First, I flew to the small island of Bali in Indonesia. From there, we flew to the island of Flores. And from there we hired a fisherman to take us in his fishing boat to tiny Komodo island, home of the Komodo dragons.

We went during the peak dry season, when the Komodo dragons head to the interior of the island, where there is water. Early the morning after we arrived, we started a big hike into the mountains. And it was then that I got my first glimpse of a wild Komodo dragon.

It's like seeing a prehistoric creature in the wild. When you are right out there in their natural habitat, there's no barrier between you and it. And if they want to chase you, they can reach quite fast speeds: Several villagers on Komodo island have been bitten. Komodo dragons are capable of hunting large prey like water buffalo and deer. They even scavenge dead animals. They are also one of the few oceangoing lizards in the world: They can swim between small islands, and they even hunt fish.

My most memorable encounter with a Komodo dragon happened at night. Besides dragons, Komodo island also happens to have the world's only blue viper (p. 126). We were out at nighttime doing something called spotlighting, which is when you walk around with a flashlight looking up into the trees. We were walking through forests and there were a lot of fallen logs. So when I was walking along and stepped on something, I thought it was a log. But instead, it happened to be the tail of a giant sleeping Komodo dragon. Komodo dragons have venom glands, and they also have saliva full of flesh-eating bacteria. But luckily this thing didn't bite me—in fact, it didn't seem to even notice that I had stepped on it!

Temnodontosaurus

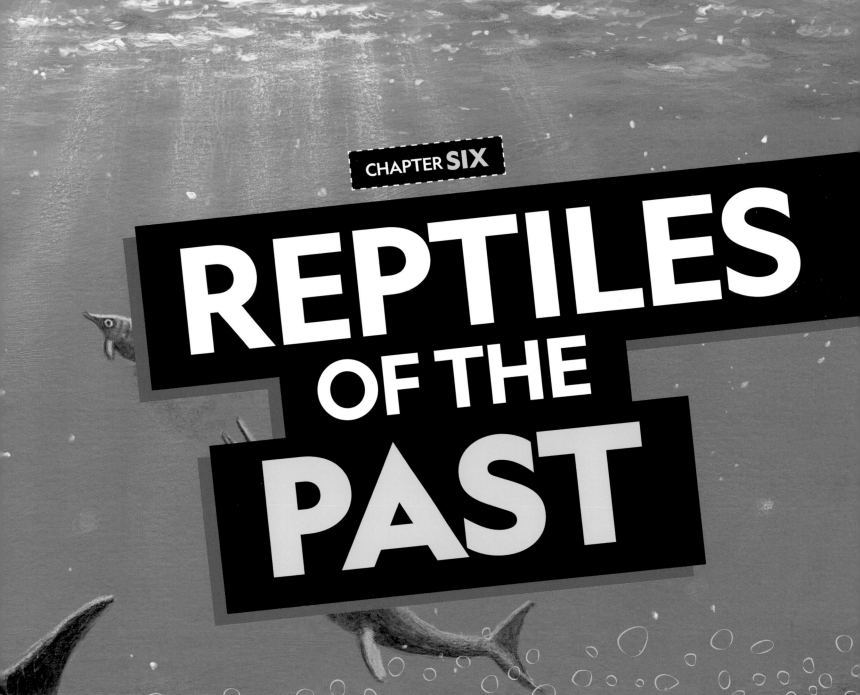

CHAPTER SIX

REPTILES
OF THE
PAST

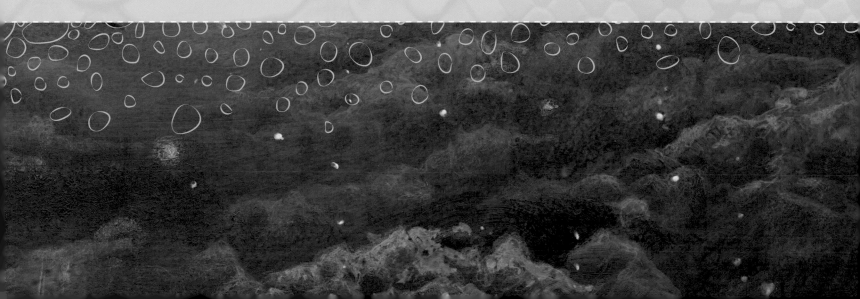

>>> **AWE-INSPIRING REPTILES ROAM OUR PLANET TODAY.** The Komodo dragon is powerful enough to take down a full-grown water buffalo. The deadly black mamba can slither faster than most people can run. Some lizards run on water and others can turn a rainbow of colors.

   But the reptiles of today pale in comparison to their ancient ancestors. Extinct reptiles include some of the biggest, baddest animals to ever roam our planet. From a snake the size of a school bus to a flying reptile as big as a fighter jet, meet these scaly beasts of the prehistoric.

MEET DREADNOUGHTUS

It was one of the largest animals to ever walk Earth. Weighing about 130,000 pounds (60,000 kg), it was heavier than a Boeing 737 airplane, or seven *Tyrannosaurus rex* put together. That massive size meant it had no predators, and is the reason for its name: *Dreadnoughtus*, meaning "fear nothing."

Growing Up

Scientists are basing their giant size estimates of *Dreadnoughtus* off only one fossil specimen that was discovered with almost complete limbs. But they know that the 65-ton (59-t) dinosaur was still growing. Its final adult size would have been even bigger!

Group Activity

Long-necked dinosaurs like *Dreadnoughtus* laid their eggs in huge colonies. Experts estimate that hundreds or thousands of these mega-dinos would have gathered together to nest.

No Noggin

So far, scientists have yet to discover a *Dreadnoughtus* skull. But scientists estimate it was tiny, relative to the animal's giant size—probably about the size of a horse's head.

Pass the Plants

This giant dino may sound scary, but *Dreadnoughtus* was a peaceful plant-eater. Experts think it would have had to spend basically every waking moment snacking to fuel its giant body.

Back Off

If an especially brave attacker did come too close for comfort, *Dreadnoughtus* likely used its huge, muscular tail or powerful hind kick to protect itself.

OCEAN GIANTS

>>> **LONG AGO, REPTILES—IN THE FORM OF DINOSAURS—RULED THE LAND.** But reptiles dominated the ancient seas, too. Called marine reptiles, they included some of the largest and most dangerous creatures that have ever lived.

Mosasaurus

Sometimes called the *T. rex* of the seas, the first *Mosasaurus* fossils were discovered in the 1760s, before people knew that dinosaurs had existed. So no one knew what to think of the bones of these gigantic sea lizards. Now scientists know that mosasaurs were a group of predators that lived in all the world's oceans. Some snacked on shellfish while others chased down fish, using their sharklike tails to propel themselves through the water at high speed. Some mosasaurs were about 56 feet (17 m) long, making these hunters about the size of a modern sperm whale.

Liopleurodon

Now this is what you call a sea monster. An ancient relative of the crocodile, *Liopleurodon* (LIE-oh-PLOOR-oh-don) could grow to up to 30 feet (9 m) long. Its huge jaws were filled with teeth up to three inches (8 cm) long. Experts think these animals were at the top of their food chain, feasting on crocodylians, plesiosaurs, turtles, and fish.

Elasmosaurus

With a quick flick of its long neck, *Elasmosaurus* could snatch up an unsuspecting fish before it even knew the huge predator was nearby. This marine reptile powered its nearly 40-foot (12-m) body through the ocean with four huge flippers. The first specimen of *Elasmosaurus* ever discovered was found in Kansas, U.S.A. Long ago, an enormous sea covered this area.

Temnodontosaurus

This was one oceangoing hunter you would not want on your tail. Larger and longer than a double-decker bus, it was probably one of the biggest ocean predators to ever exist. *Temnodontosaurus*, or "cutting-tooth lizard," used eyes the size of footballs to find prey, and giant jaws filled with razor-sharp teeth to tear them apart. It terrorized Earth's seas about 200 million years ago.

MEET TITANOBOA

About 60 million years ago, a truly unbelievable predator slithered through the tropics of South America. Longer than a school bus at nearly 50 feet (15 m), the *Titanoboa* snake was longer than any giant snake dreamed up by moviemakers—and it was 100 percent real.

Big Appetite

Experts believe this monster snake probably hunted by waiting at the water's edge until prey wandered close. Then *Titanoboa* would wrap its huge body around its meal and squeeze it to death, just like its modern relatives, the boas and anacondas.

Green anaconda

Supersize

Today, the green anaconda rules *Titanoboa*'s old stomping grounds: the swampy waters of what is now Colombia. It's the largest modern snake, at up to 550 pounds (230 kg), but that's nothing compared to *Titanoboa*, which could reach a whopping 2,500 pounds (1,130 kg).

Life at the Limits

Before *Titanoboa* was discovered, reptile experts debated how big a snake could possibly get. Their guess? Less than 40 feet (12 m)—much smaller than this real-life super snake!

Heat Seeker

Today, the largest snakes live in Earth's warmest regions, near the tropics. The same was true in *Titanoboa*'s time. Experts believe that the snake's enormous dimensions are a clue that temperatures along Earth's Equator were once much hotter—an average of about 91°F (33°C).

Equator

LOOK UP!

>>> "FLYING" SNAKES AND LIZARDS ZOOM THROUGH FORESTS IN PARTS OF OUR PLANET, BUT THEY'RE REALLY GLIDERS— NO TRUE FLYING REPTILES INHABIT EARTH TODAY. But travel back to the time of the dinosaurs, and things were different. Winged reptiles called pterosaurs, some enormous in size, terrorized the sky.

Quetzalcoatlus northropi

The largest flying animal ever discovered, *Quetzalcoatlus northropi* was almost as tall as a giraffe and had the wingspan of an F-16 fighter plane. When this massive creature was on the ground, scientists think it folded its wings up like umbrellas and walked on its front knuckles. It would launch its huge bulk into the air using all four limbs. Once airborne, this giant flier would hunt for its favorite snack—probably baby dinosaurs.

Tapejara

Today, the rainforests of Brazil are home to some of the planet's most colorful birds. But they weren't the first flamboyant flying creatures to live there. *Tapejara* was a pterosaur known for the enormous, brightly colored crest on top of its head. This creature possibly used its crest as a kind of "sail" to help it fly. But more likely, *Tapejara's* brilliant head-gear, like that of modern birds, helped it attract a mate.

Pteranodon longiceps

This mega-flier, with a wingspan up to 20 feet (6 m) across, probably spent most of its time soaring over the ocean on the hunt for fish below. For decades after it was found, *Pteranodon longiceps* was the largest known pterosaur. But before long, new discoveries blew its record away.

Nemicolopterus crypticus

Not all pterosaurs were big: *Nemicolopterus crypticus* could have fit in the palm of your hand. This creature lived in the forest of what is now northeastern China, where it used curved feet ideal for gripping tree branches. This mini pterosaur probably survived on a diet of insects, like many modern birds do today.

Coloborhynchus

Many pterosaurs were toothless, using their beaks to scoop up prey like modern storks do. But not *Coloborhynchus*. This flying reptile used jaws tipped in sharp teeth to snap at prey as it zoomed low over the water's surface. If that isn't scary enough, it was huge, sporting a wingspan of about 23 feet (7 m). Fortunately, *Coloborhynchus* likely survived on a diet of fish.

MEET ARCHELON

Leatherback turtles are the largest turtles in the world today, averaging about six feet (1.8 m) long. That's big—but it's tiny compared to *Archelon*, the biggest turtle known to have ever existed. It could reach about 13 feet (4 m) long and nearly 16 feet (5 m) across—bigger than a car!

Extra Armor

It might seem like a giant, armored turtle wouldn't have predators. But *Archelon* shared the ocean with some scary beasts, including *Mosasaurus* (p. 138) and supersize sharks. That may be why this turtle had four star-shaped plates on its underside. Experts believe these could have helped the turtle survive attacks from below.

Superb Specimen

Because conditions have to be absolutely perfect to create a fossil, many species are known from just a few bone fragments. So scientists were stunned when they discovered an amazingly complete *Archelon* fossil—missing only its skull and right front paddle—in what is now South Dakota, U.S.A.

Favorite Food

Like a modern leatherback turtle, *Archelon* probably used its hooked beak to dine on soft creatures such as jellyfish. It snipped their bodies into pieces, then gobbled those up.

Don't Sink

Also like a modern leatherback, *Archelon* had only a thin outer covering instead of a hefty shell. That's probably because a hard shell would have weighed down a creature of *Archelon*'s huge size, making it difficult for the giant turtle to stay afloat as it navigated the ancient seas.

Leatherback turtle

REPTILE BITES

Scientists now think that most two-legged dinosaurs **HAD FEATHERS.**

Ampelosaurus was a 50-foot (15-m)-long dinosaur—but its brain was only **A LITTLE BIGGER THAN A WALNUT.**

There are about 10,000 species of dinosaurs alive today. **WE CALL THEM BIRDS.**

MORE THAN 1,000 SPECIES of dinosaurs have been discovered.

Dinosaurs were reptiles. But reptiles also ruled Earth before dinosaurs evolved. One reptile, *Garjainia,* looked like

A MODERN-DAY KOMODO DRAGON.

In an 80-million-year-old fossil, a *Velociraptor* and a *Protoceratops* are

LOCKED IN A DINOSAUR DEATH MATCH.

Scientists think the fighting dinosaurs were buried by a sudden sand flow, then were fossilized.

Hadrosaurs had

AS MANY AS 1,400 TEETH—

ideal for grinding up plants.

Titanosaurs were so big that they could have peeked inside

A FIFTH-FLOOR WINDOW.

Tyrannosaurus rex had jaws powerful enough to

CRUSH A CAR.

FACE-TO-FACE

WITH CAVE-DWELLING CROCODILES

THERE IS AN AMAZING PLACE IN WESTERN AUSTRALIA CALLED TUNNEL CREEK NATIONAL PARK. There, a creek flows right into this cave system that is nearly half a mile (750 m) long. And this dark underground creek is crawling with life, including Australian freshwater crocodiles. It's one of the few places anywhere in the world where you can find crocodiles inside a cave.

This cave is interesting for other reasons, too. It is one of the oldest caves in Western Australia, and it's an important ecosystem for lots of animals. It is also an important place for Aboriginal people: It has ancient rock art, and was also a famous hideout for an Aboriginal freedom fighter named Jandamarra. But I was there to see the crocodiles.

This cave is a very spooky place. You have to wade through the water to cross the cave, and you know there are crocodiles in that water. This species isn't known to harm humans, but then again, not a lot of humans tempt fate by wading into these waters!

Being cold-blooded animals, crocodiles need sunlight to function properly. But of course, there is no sunlight in most of this cave. So instead, this population has adapted a totally different way of maintaining body temperature. They are able to warm their bodies using geothermal energy: hot water that seeps from the heated rocks surrounding the cave into the creek here. It's like they are living in a hot tub! The cave is full of crayfish, catfish, and other water-living animals. So the crocodiles have a plentiful supply of food.

Most crocodiles inside the cave are about five feet (1.5 m) long, but a couple are close to 6.6 feet (2 m), which is quite big for this species. We have tagged them so we can identify individuals and see how they are growing and moving around as time passes. What we are seeing is that the same set of about eight crocodiles is always found within this cave. Why do they choose to live here when they could easily move to the creek or water pools outside? As we keep studying them, we hope to find out!

Hawksbill turtle

CHAPTER SEVEN

SUPER CREATURES

>>> **REPTILES INCLUDE SOME OF THE MOST EXTREME SPECIES ON EARTH.** They strike at prey with toxic bites, reach enormous sizes, and some live longer than most other animals.

In this chapter, you'll meet some record-holding reptiles. There are creatures as long as an elephant, and species so small they could perch on the head of a match. There are species that dive into the deep sea and species that live on the highest peaks of mountains—and many more besides!

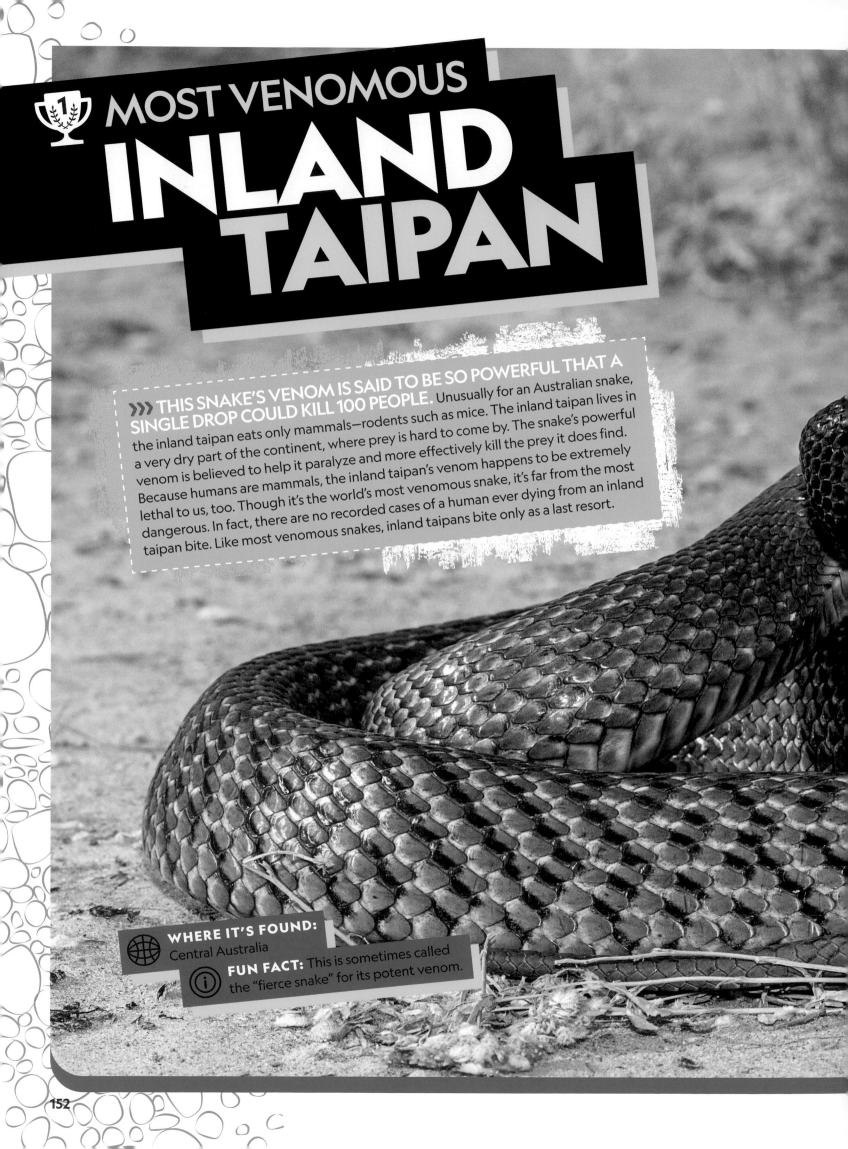

MOST VENOMOUS
INLAND TAIPAN

>>> **THIS SNAKE'S VENOM IS SAID TO BE SO POWERFUL THAT A SINGLE DROP COULD KILL 100 PEOPLE.** Unusually for an Australian snake, the inland taipan eats only mammals—rodents such as mice. The inland taipan lives in a very dry part of the continent, where prey is hard to come by. The snake's powerful venom is believed to help it paralyze and more effectively kill the prey it does find. Because humans are mammals, the inland taipan's venom happens to be extremely lethal to us, too. Though it's the world's most venomous snake, it's far from the most dangerous. In fact, there are no recorded cases of a human ever dying from an inland taipan bite. Like most venomous snakes, inland taipans bite only as a last resort.

WHERE IT'S FOUND:
Central Australia

FUN FACT: This is sometimes called the "fierce snake" for its potent venom.

② RUNNER-UP: BEAKED SEA SNAKE

Sea snakes are among the most venomous snakes on Earth, and the beaked sea snake, found in South and Southeast Asia, is considered the deadliest of them all. Experts estimate that its venom is several times more lethal than a cobra's. It is also the only sea snake for which an antivenom is available.

BIGGEST
SALTWATER CROCODILE

WHERE IT'S FOUND: Coastal and tidal areas of the eastern Indian and western Pacific Oceans

FUN FACT: This croc can live in both freshwater and salt water.

>>> **IT'S THE LARGEST LIVING REPTILE.** Although there are tales of extremely large "salties" reaching more than 30 feet (9 m) in length, the biggest one ever caught and actually measured is about 20 feet (6 m) long. The famous crocodile, named Lolong, was caught in Mindanao in the Philippines. Because crocodiles grow continuously throughout their whole lives, giants like Lolong are likely quite old. Saltwater crocodiles lurk by the water's edge, waiting for prey to meander near. Then the crocodile strikes, lunging for and dragging prey underwater to drown it. Saltwater crocodiles are so big that they can eat just about anything, from pigs to full-grown buffalo.

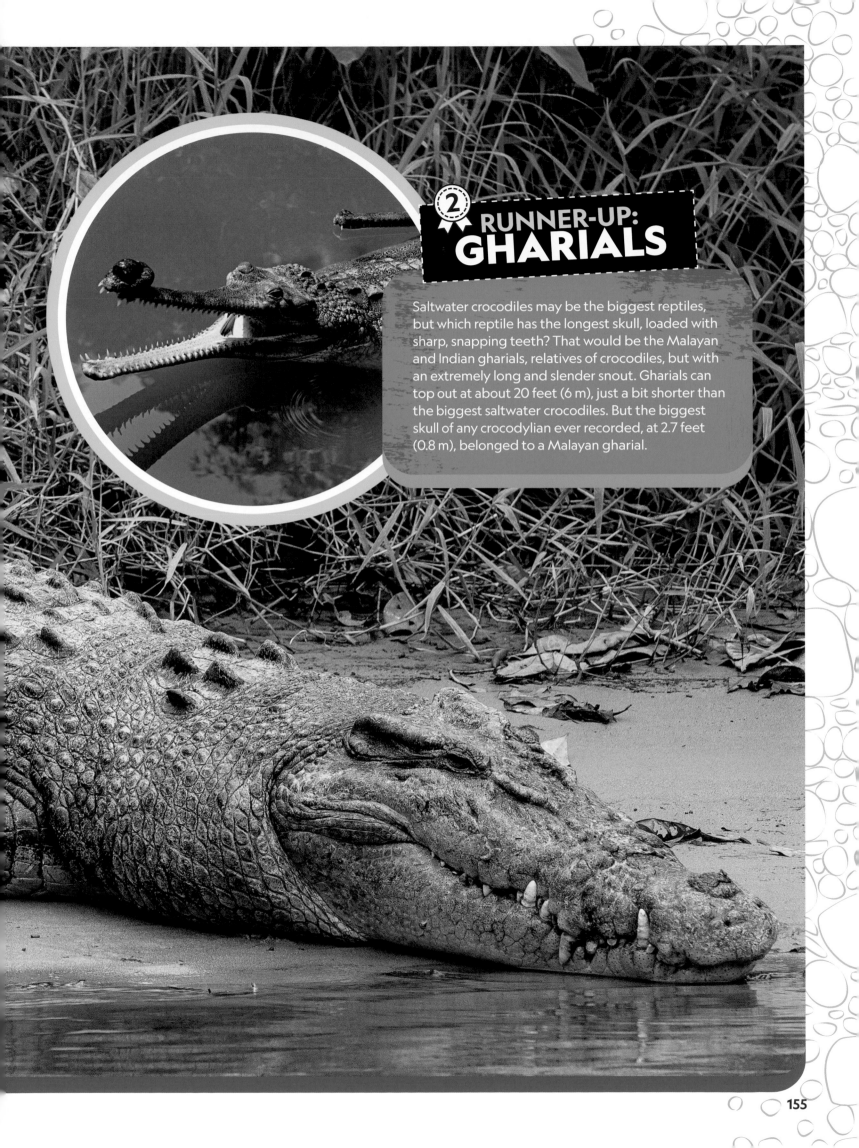

② RUNNER-UP: GHARIALS

Saltwater crocodiles may be the biggest reptiles, but which reptile has the longest skull, loaded with sharp, snapping teeth? That would be the Malayan and Indian gharials, relatives of crocodiles, but with an extremely long and slender snout. Gharials can top out at about 20 feet (6 m), just a bit shorter than the biggest saltwater crocodiles. But the biggest skull of any crocodylian ever recorded, at 2.7 feet (0.8 m), belonged to a Malayan gharial.

SMALLEST
NANO CHAMELEON

WHERE IT'S FOUND: A small part of northern Madagascar

FUN FACT: Nano chameleons hide from predators at night by clinging to blades of grass.

>>> **THIS CHAMELEON—*BROOKESIA NANA*, ALSO CALLED THE NANO CHAMELEON— IS ABOUT THE SIZE OF A SUNFLOWER SEED, SO SMALL IT CAN COMFORTABLY SIT ON A HUMAN FINGERTIP.** This miniature creature was discovered in 2021, when scientists were exploring a rainforest in the island of Madagascar. It's so tiny that experts think it survives on a diet of mites and springtails, creatures so small many can be seen only with a microscope.

② RUNNER-UP: BARBADOS THREADSNAKE

Curled up, it can fit on a quarter. The Barbados threadsnake is the world's smallest snake at just four inches (10 cm) long and about as thick as a strand of spaghetti. It's so small that it can't chomp on anything other than the teeniest of prey. Even large ants and termites are often too big, so the snake mostly survives by eating ant and termite eggs.

WHERE IT'S FOUND:
Southeast Asia

FUN FACT: Wild reticulated pythons sometimes eat deer and boars.

① LONGEST

RETICULATED PYTHON

>>> THE WORLD RECORD FOR THE LONGEST SNAKE IN CAPTIVITY EVER MEASURED GOES TO MEDUSA, A RETICULATED PYTHON THAT WAS MORE THAN 25 FEET (7.7 M) LONG. That's longer than a giraffe is tall! Captive reptiles, with their regular diet and protection from predators, can get much bigger than wild ones. Wild reticulated pythons are much smaller, regularly reaching lengths of more than 16 feet (4.9 m). That's still one long snake!

② RUNNERS-UP:
BURMESE PYTHON & GREEN ANACONDA

It's tough for experts to say for sure which snake species is the longest. For one thing, it's likely that humans have simply never spotted the world's longest wild snake. For another thing, measuring a giant, slithering predator properly is not easy! Besides reticulated pythons, other superlong snakes include the Burmese python, which can grow to more than 18 feet (5.5 m), and the green anaconda, which can grow to similar lengths.

Burmese python

Green anaconda

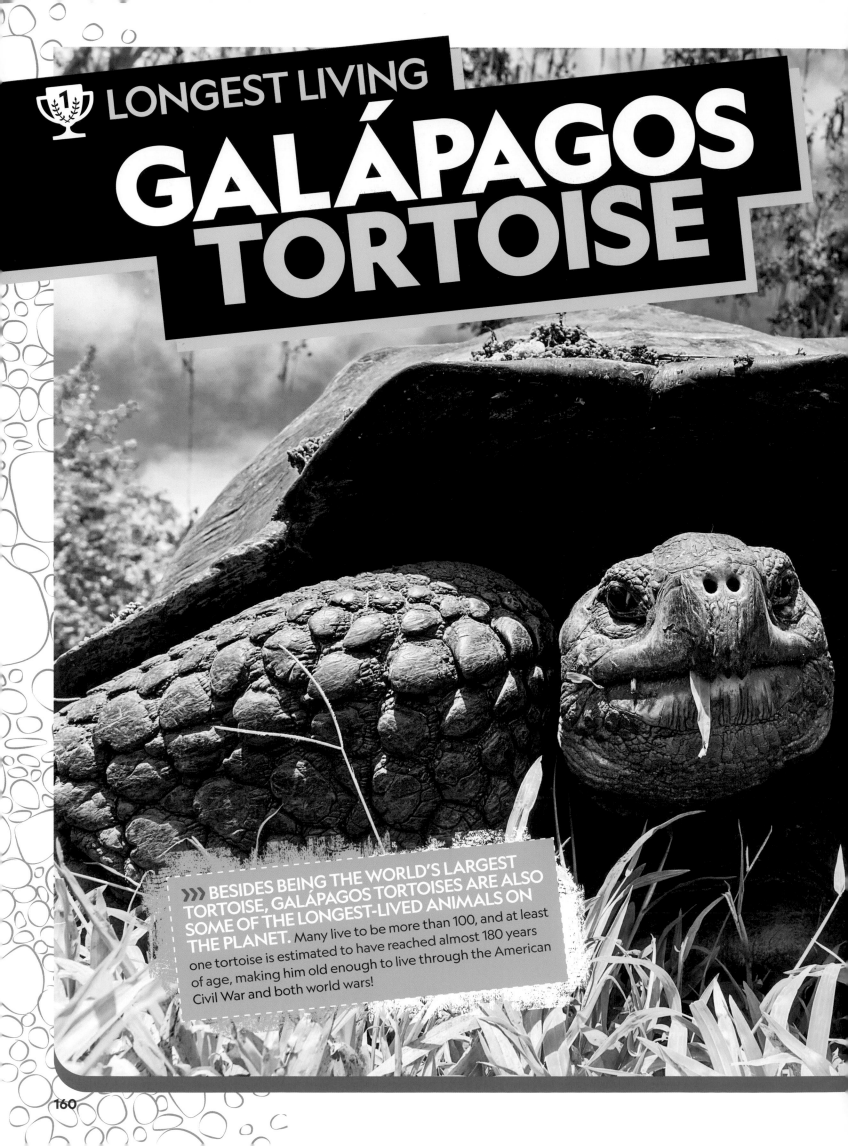

LONGEST LIVING
GALÁPAGOS TORTOISE

>>> BESIDES BEING THE WORLD'S LARGEST TORTOISE, GALÁPAGOS TORTOISES ARE ALSO SOME OF THE LONGEST-LIVED ANIMALS ON THE PLANET. Many live to be more than 100, and at least one tortoise is estimated to have reached almost 180 years of age, making him old enough to live through the American Civil War and both world wars!

RUNNER-UP: TUATARA

This rare reptile, found only in New Zealand, is not only a living fossil whose species has survived on Earth since the time of the dinosaurs—it is also one of the planet's longest-lived animals. Experts think that wild tuataras can live to be about 100 years old.

WHERE IT'S FOUND:
Galápagos Islands

FUN FACT: Galápagos tortoises have air chambers inside their shells that help decrease the shells' weight to lighten the tortoise's load.

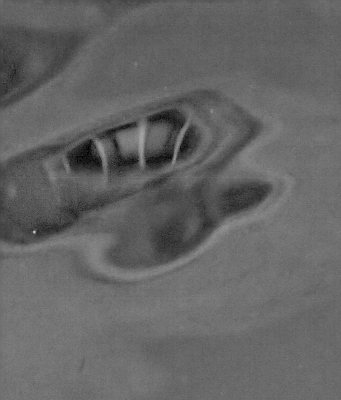

Yellow-bellied
sea snake

"There are about 75 different species of sea snakes in the world, and this is the only one that is completely pelagic, meaning that it spends its entire life in the open ocean away from the coral reefs and shallow waters. Most sea snakes rub against rocks or coral when it's time for them to shed. But in the open ocean, there's nothing to rub against. So this one is 'knotting,' rubbing its skin against itself to shed. I photographed the snake from under-water so what you are seeing on top is its reflection at the water surface. Spotting this behavior was a case of lucky timing."
—Ru Somaweera

DEEPEST DIVER
LEATHERBACK TURTLE

>>> EQUIPPED WITH WET SUITS, MASKS, AND OXYGEN TANKS, HUMAN SCUBA DIVERS ROUTINELY DIVE TO ABOUT 100 FEET (30 M). Without any tools to assist it, the leatherback turtle crushes this record, capable of diving to an astounding 4,200 feet (1,280 m)—though most of the time, they dive to about 650 feet (200 m). That record dive is about as deep as 14 Statues of Liberty stacked on top of each other! Although human divers can suffer decompression sickness, caused by bubbles of nitrogen gas in their tissues when breathing underwater, leatherbacks don't have this problem. That's because they dive on one breath of air, and also because their leathery shell absorbs nitrogen. Cool trick!

WHERE IT'S FOUND: Ocean waters worldwide, except near poles

FUN FACT: Leatherbacks spend almost their entire lives at sea—only females come to land, to lay their eggs.

② RUNNER-UP: SEA SNAKES

Snakes can slither across the ground, glide through the air ... and even dive into the deep sea! In 2019, a team of Australian scientists recorded sea snakes swimming at about 800 feet (245 m) below the ocean's surface. The scientists were shocked. Though sea snakes are excellent swimmers and capable of holding their breath for possibly as long as eight hours, they mostly stick to shallow waters.

1

FASTEST

BLACK MAMBA

>>> THE BLACK MAMBA IS FEARED THROUGHOUT ITS HOMELAND OF SOUTH-ERN AND EASTERN AFRICA, AND FOR GOOD REASON. Its venom is so toxic that it's said two drops are enough to kill a human. It can be highly aggressive when threatened. And it can slither faster than many humans can run, reaching speeds of up to 12 miles an hour (19 km/h) over short distances. The black mamba is widely regarded as the fastest snake in the world, but it's tough to say for sure: When faced with an angry snake, most people don't stop to clock its speed!

FUN FACT: Black mambas are actually olive or brown in color. They get their name from the black inside of their mouth, which they open wide when under threat.

② RUNNER-UP: VIPERS

Some snakes don't just move fast—they also strike fast. A striking snake can whip its head forward so quickly that it experiences more than 20 g-forces—about six times what an astronaut feels during liftoff! It's tough to say for sure which species has the fastest strike of all. But many experts think the record goes to vipers—a family that includes rattlesnakes and copperheads. These snakes can lunge forward about half a foot (15 cm) in only 70 milliseconds. That's about three times faster than the blink of an eye!

REPTILE BITES

Of the 23 species of crocodylians, seven are **CRITICALLY ENDANGERED.**

Chameleons can **COIL THEIR TAILS AROUND TREE BRANCHES** to help them hang on.

A chameleon's tongue is more than **TWICE AS LONG AS ITS BODY.**

Snakes have been recorded **EATING CROCODILES, DEER, AND COWS.**

The saw-scaled viper is thought to **KILL MORE PEOPLE WITHIN ITS RANGE** than all other venomous snakes combined.

Some species of skinks are **BORN WITH BLUE TAILS.** The color helps distract predators when the skinks drop their tails.

Some lizards **EAT THEIR SHED SKIN.**

The scales on a turtle's shell are **CALLED SCUTES.**

The inner layer of a turtle's shell is made of **UP TO 60 CONNECTED BONES.**

The name "tuatara" comes from a **MAORI PHRASE MEANING "PEAKS ON THE BACK,"** referring to the row of raised scales on their backs.

FACE-TO-FACE

WITH AN AFRICAN DWARF CROCODILE

I HAVE SEEN ALL THE LARGEST SPECIES OF CROCODYLIANS IN THE WORLD: THE SALTWATER CROCODILE, THE AMERICAN ALLIGATOR, THE NILE CROCODILE, AND THE MALAYAN GHARIAL. But I haven't seen most of the smallest species. They are actually quite tricky to find. For one thing, they only live in very isolated parts of the world. And unlike big crocodiles, small ones are very shy and secretive. Also, some of them live in jungle streams full of vegetation compared to in open rivers or wetlands like the big ones. So as a crocodile lover, seeing the smallest species is a big deal.

The African dwarf crocodile lives in tiny tropical forest streams of western Africa. And they only grow to be about five feet (1.5 m) at maximum, and up to about 66 pounds (30 kg) in weight. So in the crocodile world, they are miniature. Finding them is very difficult, even when you are right in their habitat. They are known to live in large burrows, and they hide themselves in the reeds along riverbanks and among tree roots.

Finally, I was lucky enough to spot one. They are very interesting-looking because they are really heavily armored. Crocodile skin has what's called osteoderms—tiny bone particles within the skin. Some species don't have many osteoderms, so their skin is smoother and more flexible. But some crocodiles—especially the tiny ones, because they have a lot of predators—have a lot. The scientific name of the African dwarf crocodile actually means "bony throat," because its neck especially is very heavily armored. That's because some of their predators, such as big cats, attack by biting the neck.

It was a very cool thing, seeing the smallest species of croc on Earth. But this photo is from a zoom lens—I was quite far away from it. I have touched the four largest species of crocodylians, but I still have yet to touch the smallest. Someday, I hope to!

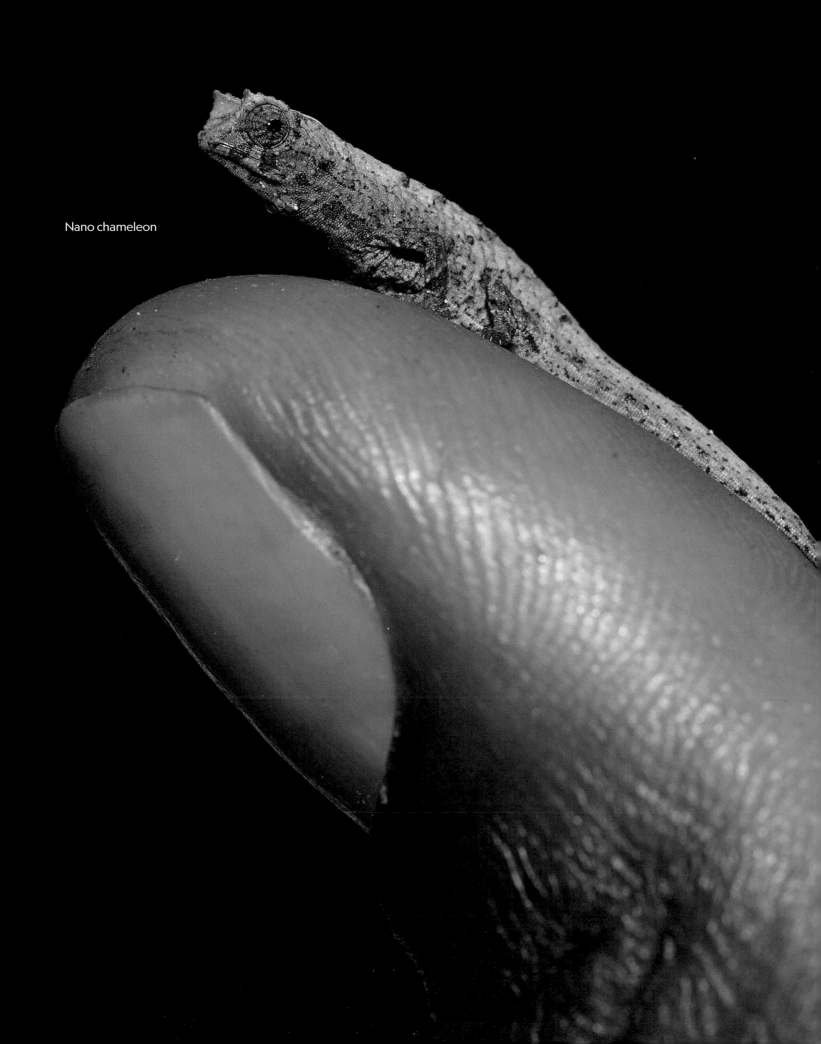

Nano chameleon

CHAPTER EIGHT

SAVING SPECIES

>>> **THOUGH HUMANS HAVE CLIMBED TO THE TOP OF EARTH'S HIGHEST MOUNTAINS AND THE BOTTOM OF ITS DEEPEST SEAS, THERE IS STILL MUCH TO BE DISCOVERED ON THE PLANET WE CALL HOME.** Reptile scientists, called herpetologists, are constantly finding new species of snakes, lizards, turtles, and crocodylians. And they think there are thousands more reptiles out there, hiding everywhere from deserts to rainforests, just waiting to be discovered.

But as scientists have learned more about reptiles, they've also learned that these creatures are some of the most threatened on the planet. Reptiles face a host of problems, from the loss of their habitat to being plucked out of the wild to be sold as pets. But there's still time to protect these animals and make sure they have a home on Earth.

EARLESS MONITOR LIZARD

 WHERE IT'S FOUND:
Borneo

 FUN FACT: Earless monitor lizards get their name from their lack of ear openings.

>>> IN 2008, A TEAM OF SCIENTISTS WAS TREKKING THROUGH THE JUNGLE IN BORNEO WHEN THEY HAPPENED UPON SOMETHING ODD: A BROWN LIZARD WITH BRIGHT BLUE EYES THAT LOOKED LIKE A MINIATURE DRAGON. It was an earless monitor lizard, a very rarely seen reptile. The team published their discovery and included the rough location where they had spotted the lizard. That turned out to be a mistake. Reptile collectors started scouring the jungle for the lizard, and soon earless monitor lizards started showing up in online ads. The lizards sold for as much as $25,000. By announcing their discovery, scientists had accidentally set off a frenzy of people looking to own the rare reptile as a pet. Now scientists fear that so many earless monitors will be taken from the wild that the animal will soon be extinct.

REPTILES AT RISK

Reptiles first appeared on Earth about 300 million years ago and ruled the planet for millennia. But now many of them face grave danger. Experts estimate that about one out of every five reptile species is currently at risk of going extinct. Here are the biggest threats they face today.

Habitat Destruction

The biggest danger reptiles face is the loss of their homeland. As the human population expands, people clear forests and divert water sources to make room for houses and farms. This destroys the habitat many reptiles depend on for survival. Experts believe that to prevent an enormous loss of reptile species, we have to take actions, such as protecting wildlands.

Reptiles as Food

Humans around the world rely on reptiles as an important source of food. People generally don't eat enough of most species of crocodylians, snakes, and lizards to put them at risk. The exception is turtles. So many turtles are collected for food that they are now the most threatened group of reptiles on the planet, with more than 60 percent of species either threatened or already extinct.

Climate Change

Reptiles rely on their environment to regulate their temperature, basking in the sun to keep warm and retreating to the shade to cool down. Because of this, they are especially sensitive to temperature shifts caused by climate change. Scientists fear that as the world continues to heat up, reptiles could face all kinds of challenges. One of the biggest problems is that for some reptiles, the temperature of the eggs' environment determines the sex of the hatchlings. In sea turtles, for example, eggs that incubate below 81.8°F (27.7°C) become male. Eggs that incubate above 87.8°F (31°C) become female. Research shows that changing temperatures are now causing issues with the ratio of males to females. That could make it difficult for this species to survive.

Pet Trade

Easy to care for and fun to watch, many reptiles make great pets. Some are bred in captivity just to live a life in the care of humans. But many others are plucked from their homes in the wild and sold illegally. In one 2020 study, experts found that about half of reptiles bought and sold online were captured from the wild, mostly illegally. Social media has worsened the problem, by exposing reptile owners to exotic new species to add to their collections.

SMUGGLED SPECIES

>>> ON THE INTERNET, ADS SHOW PHOTOS OF SNAKES PATTERNED IN JEWEL COLORS AND LIZARDS THAT LOOK MORE LIKE DRAGONS THAN REAL-LIFE REPTILES.

Some of these animals are snatched from their wild homes and sold illegally, an industry called wildlife trafficking. Here are some reptiles under threat.

Leopard Tortoise

Along with lions and elephants, leopard tortoises are a signature animal of the African savanna, easy to spot by their domed shells marked with a bold black-and-yellow pattern. Unfortunately, this pattern makes these animals attractive as pets and also for industries that turn their shells into decorative items. Though they are a protected species, the number of leopard tortoises captured and carried out of their homeland has skyrocketed in recent years. Smugglers use all kinds of clever tactics to hide the animals: One traveler was even caught trying to sneak a leopard tortoise through the Singapore border in a sunglasses case.

Harlequin Gecko

It's no wonder that this gecko attracts the attention of reptile collectors, with its intricate pattern of browns, oranges, and greens. The harlequin gecko lives only on Rakiura, also called Stewart Island, an island south of New Zealand. Due to the geckos' dwindling numbers and remote location, scientists know very little about this endangered animal. And although it is illegal to bring them out of New Zealand, smugglers do anyway.

Blood Python

In the wild, this snake is a stealthy hunter. It holds perfectly still as it hides in water or under leaves, using heat-sensing pits on its upper lip to detect when prey comes close. But the snake's camouflage is no match for smugglers, who use its skins to make leather. Every year, about 50,000 blood python skins are exported from Indonesia alone.

Chinese Crocodile Lizard

Chinese crocodile lizards are often removed from their homeland in southern China and northern Vietnam to become pets. Collectors like these animals because they look prehistoric—and that's because they are. Chinese crocodile lizards evolved more than 100 million years ago, around the time birds first emerged. They are the last surviving members of a family called Shinisauridae. But experts fear that no more than about 1,000 of these ancient reptiles may still be alive today.

Asiatic Softshell Turtle

The Asiatic softshell turtle, native to Southeast Asia, spends much of its time buried in silt at the bottom of lakes and rivers, its elongated snout poking out for breathing. This turtle has few natural predators—smooth-coated otters and tigers mainly prey on adults of this species. The biggest danger to this turtle comes from an unnatural predator: humans. So many Asiatic softshell turtles are collected as food in their home of Southeast Asia that they are now vulnerable to extinction.

"Spotting this tuatara was a highlight in my career. We have nearly 12,000 reptiles in the world. Out of all of these, this guy is the only one that has an entire scientific order for himself—that's how unusual it is. That means it is extremely different from any other living reptile. On top of that, it's only found in New Zealand and it's threatened and extremely rare. It's a living fossil, the last survivor of a line of reptiles that dates back to 200 million years ago."

—Ru Somaweera

CONSERVATION HEROES!

Human activity may be threatening reptiles all across the planet. But humans can be reptiles' biggest protectors, too. Meet five wildlife warriors who are saving reptile species from South America to Sri Lanka.

Father of Turtles

Biologist and activist Tomas Diagne has a nickname: Africa's "Father of Turtles." That's because he has spent more than 20 years working to save threatened and endangered turtles, tortoises, and terrapins—which together form a group called chelonians. Diagne founded the "Village des Tortues" (Tortoise Village) in Senegal as a place to breed threatened and endangered species in captivity and then return them to the wild. It soon became a place where people in the community could interact with these animals—and learn to care about their survival along the way.

Protected Place

In order to protect reptiles, it's vital to protect the places they live. That's the idea behind Masungi Georeserve, a roughly 1,000-acre (410-ha) reserve in Rizal, a province in the Philippines. Conservationist Ann Dumaliang has devoted her life to protecting Masungi and the wildlife that calls it home. Within the park is a karst, an unusual type of landscape situated on top of limestone that has weathered away to create dramatic ridges, towers, sinkholes, and caves. This area is a hot spot for reptiles: the Philippine pit viper, Philippine cobra, Kalinga narrowmouth frog, and Philippine flying dragon all call this place home. There aren't just reptiles there: The reserve is home to prehistoric plants older than dinosaurs!

Reptile Rescuer

Anslem de Silva started out as a magician. But today, instead of trying to make coins or cards vanish, he's trying to prevent Sri Lanka's reptiles from disappearing. He works to educate the people of Sri Lanka about the reptiles that share their homeland by publishing books that bust myths and share facts about these animals. De Silva also holds conferences and organizes exhibitions so that people can meet the reptiles face-to-face.

Fighting Back

In 1935, officials released cane toads, which are native to South and Central America—to Australia. They hoped the toads would help control the populations of beetles that destroyed sugarcane crops. Unfortunately, the toads showed no interest in the beetles. But they did multiply until more than 200 million of them were hopping across Australia, spreading disease and killing the snakes, lizards, and crocodiles that eat them. That was devastating for reptile biologist Georgia Ward-Fear to watch. So she found a way to protect native reptiles: She trains them to keep away from the toads by giving them small doses of cane toad toxin before the invasion arrives in an area, teaching them that the toads are toxic, not tasty.

Caiman Comeback

In the late 1980s, the broad-snouted caiman was nearly extinct in Santa Fe Province, Argentina. But then, conservationist Alejandro Larriera and his team stepped in. They identified the last of the caiman's nesting sites and carefully collected the eggs. The team incubated the eggs under artificial lights until they hatched, then raised the babies until they were big and strong enough to survive on their own. Then the human helpers released the caimans back into their habitat. After 35 years of this work, broad-snouted caimans are once again flourishing, not just in Santa Fe but all across the country.

WHAT CAN YOU DO?

Helping save Earth's reptiles is a big job. But you don't need to be a scientist to help—in fact, you don't even need to be a grown-up!

Make a Reptile Refuge

You don't have to travel to faraway jungles to help reptiles. You can protect their habitats right in your own backyard! Rocks and logs give reptiles places to bask and live under. Native species of flowers, trees, and bushes—those original to your area—will host insects that they like to eat. No yard is too small to become a reptile habitat.

Get to Know Them

People won't fight to protect an animal if they don't know it exists. So one of the best ways to help conservationists is to learn about all of Earth's amazing reptiles and share what you discover with others, including your family and friends.

Be Responsible

Reptiles can make great pets. But if you'd like to keep a turtle or snake, make sure to do it the right way. Before you adopt your new pet, make sure to purchase only from registered pet shops and dealers who can show paperwork to prove that the animal wasn't illegally smuggled from the wild. And if you ever find that you can no longer care for your pet, never set it free outside. Released reptiles can set up new populations that wipe out native species. Your local animal shelter can help you find the right place to take reptiles.

Become a Reptile Tracker

Have you ever spotted a snake or lizard in your neighborhood and wondered what it was? Apps like iNaturalist enable users to upload photos they take of wildlife. Scientists then help identify the species in the photos. The information users collect helps scientists track where and when reptiles appear around the world.

FACE-TO-FACE

WITH A SHORT-NOSED SEA SNAKE

THIS IS ONE OF MY FAVORITE STORIES FROM ALL MY YEARS OF ADVENTURES WITH REPTILES. This particular species is called a short-nosed sea snake. And until recently, it was only known to live in two very isolated reefs off the coast of northern Western Australia, the Ashmore Reef and Hibernia Reef. Between 1998 and 2000, the entire population of these snakes vanished. For the next 15 years, we didn't see a single specimen. The Australian government officially declared it extinct.

Then, in 2015, something amazing happened: Out of the blue, short-nosed sea snakes started turning up in a totally different part of Australia, a place called Shark Bay. This is hundreds of miles away from the reefs that they were known to live in! Miraculously, the species had been rediscovered.

Three years later, I was training some fishermen in another part of Australia—Exmouth. I was teaching them how to identify different species of sea snakes so that when they accidentally caught them in their nets, they could note which species they had found and let us know after releasing them back. I told them that this snake is incredibly rare, and that they probably wouldn't see one. A couple of the fishermen told me, "It's not rare. We catch them every night." I confess that I didn't really believe them. I told them that if they caught any that night, to bring them to me the next morning, just to confirm and record. Well, the next day they brought a whole tub of snakes to me, and *three* of them were this "very rare" species, the short-nosed sea snake!

For me, it was a really eye-opening experience. Sometimes as scientists we can think that we know more than the local people do. This showed me how important it is to listen to the people who live and work every day in the area where you are doing research. If we don't talk to these people, we are missing a huge resource of information! Since then, I have had some really productive collaborations with fishermen, and I've learned a lot from them.

INDEX

Boldface indicates illustrations.

INDEX

CREDITS

All photos by Ruchira Somaweera unless otherwise noted below. *AD=Adobe Stock; SS=Shutterstock*

Front Cover: (UP LE), shanemyersphoto/AD; (UP RT), imageBROKER/AD; (LO LE), Deki/AD; (LO RT), kuritafsheen/AD; **Spine:** nonfacciofoto/AD; **Back Cover:** Cathy Keifer/SS; **Front Matter:** 1, mgkuijpers/AD; 2-3, Mieke Suharini/500px/Getty Images; 4-5 (background), Vera/AD; 4 (UP), asawinimages/SS; 4 (LO), Kjeld Friis/AD; 5, PhotogGuenter Fischer/imageBROKERrapher/SS; **Chapter One:** 8 (UP), adogslifephoto/AD; 8 (CTR LE), Coralreefart/Dreamstime; 8 (LO), Pascal Halder/AD; 9, ondrejprosicky/AD; 10 (LE), PhotogDaniel Eskridgerapher/AD; 10 (CTR), bennytrapp/AD; 10 (LO), Twin Chan/AD; 10-11 (UP), nonfacciofoto/AD; 11 (UP RT), chrisstockphotography/Alamy Stock Photo; 11 (LO), Animal Stock/Alamy Stock Photo; 14-15, Nick Blamire-Brown/SS; 16-17, WILDLIFE GmbH/Alamy Stock Photo; 18 (UP LE), Warpaint/AD; 18 (UP RT), Matt Jeppson/SS; 18, reptiles4all/SS; 19 (UP), Gaschwald/AD; 19 (CTR RT), Universal Images Group North America LLC/DeAgostini/Alamy Stock Photo; 19 (CTR), Renato/AD; 19 (LO), Mike & Valerie Mille/AD; 20-21, Matthijs Kuijpers/Dreamstime; 22-23, Daniel Heuclin/Nature Picture Library; 24-25, Lauren/AD; 28-29, Michael Patrick O'Neill/Alamy Stock Photo; 30-31, Thomp Jerry/Getty Images; 32-33, Richie/AD; 34-35, FLPA/Alamy Stock Photo; **Chapter Two:** 38-39, ChristianHerzog/AD; 40 (LO), Uryadnikov Sergey/AD; 40-41, Senk/Dreamstime; 41 (LO), twinlynx/AD; 42, imageBROKER/Alamy Stock Photo; 44-45 (UP), vaclav/AD; 44 (LO), Stu Porter/SS; 47 (UP), Judith/AD; 47 (LO), Martin Harvey/Getty Images; 48-49, NG Maps; 50 (UP LE), Dmitry/AD; 50 (CTR), mari/AD; 50 (LO), Irina K./AD; 51 (pan), Ruslan Grumble/AD; 51 (UP LE), tanoochai/SS; 51 (CTR RT), Frédéric Prochasson/AD; 51 (LO), J.K2507/SS; 52 (UP), Hemant Arun Chhatre/SS; 52 (LO), Chantelle Bosch/SS; 53 (UP LE), Ben Twist/AD; 53 (CTR), paytai/SS; 53 (LO RT), mgkuijpers/AD; 54 (CTR), phototrip.cz/AD; 55 (UP RT), mgkuijpers/AD; 55 (LO), NatalieJean/AD; 58, mgkuijpers/AD; 59 (CTR LE), mgkuijpers/AD; 59 (LO), Xinhua/Alamy Stock Photo; 60, mgkuijpers/AD; 61 (UP RT), breakingthewalls/AD; 61 (LO LE), Chris Mattison/Alamy Stock Photo; 61 (LO RT), mgkuijpers/AD; 62 (LE), wildestanimal/AD; 62 (RT), Tristan Barrington/AD; 63 (UP), miami2you/AD; 63 (croc top), Horst Bingemer/SS; 63 (croc side), Pb/AD; 63 (gator top), Bruce MacQueen/SS; 63 (gator side), Philippe/AD; 63 (LO), Rich Lindie/AD; 64 (impala), Armitar/SS; 64 (caviar), Popova Olga/AD; 64 (cactus), Binh Thanh Bui/SS; 64 (flower), nito/SS; 64 (egg), andregric/SS; 64 (cricket), maeklong/AD; 64 (spider), Papik/SS; 64 (plate), sommai/AD; 64 (LO), AfriPics/Alamy Stock Photo; 65 (UP), Samuel/AD; 65 (CTR RT), Nick Dale/Design Pics/Getty Images; 65 (LO LE), Helmut Göthel Symbiosis/Alamy Stock Photo; 65 (CTR LE), taviphoto/AD; 65 (LO RT), FunnyDive/SS; **Chapter Three:** 68-69, Chien Lee/Minden Pictures; 70-71, 25ehaag6/AD; 74, Stephen Dalton/Nature Picture Library; 75 (UP), Cede Prudente/Avalon; 75 (LO), I Wayan Sumatika/AD; 78 (UP LE), VivianGiselle/AD; 78 (UP RT), Lindsey Swierk; 78 (LO), davidcarbo/AD; 79 (UP), Mark Kostich/AD; 79 (LO LE), Sandesh Kadur/Nature Picture Library; 79 (LO RT), Cathy Keifer/AD; 80, PhotogGuenter Fischer/imageBROKERrapher/SS; 81 (UP), Lee Eui-Zun/SS; 81 (CTR), Soumabrata Moulick/AD; 82 (UP), Nick Greaves; Agfa Awards Winner/Alamy Stock Photo; 83 (UP), Ed Reschke/Getty Images; 83 (LO), Huw Cordey/Nature Picture Library; 84-85, Bence Mate/Nature Picture Library; 86, mgkuijpers/AD; 87 (LO), Yvette Cardozo/Alamy Stock Photo; 88 (LO), Etienne Littlefair/Nature Picture Library; **Chapter Four:** 90-91, Uryadnikov Sergey/AD; 92-93, blickwinkel/Alamy Stock Photo; 94-95, Uryadnikov Sergey/AD; 96, mgkuijpers/AD; 97 (UP), MichaelL/AD; 97 (CTR RT), Clément Carbillet/Biosphoto; 97 (LO), Ken Griffiths/AD; 98-99, mgkuijpers/AD; 100-101, Rodger Klein/Blue Planet Archive; 102 (UP), Jan/AD; 102 (LO), Sebastian/AD; 103 (UP), Sinclair Stammers/Science Source; 103 (CTR LE), John Cancalosi/Nature Picture Library; 103 (CTR RT), Willem Van Zyl/AD; 103 (LO), prin79/AD; 104-105, Sista/AD; 106-108-109, mgkuijpers/AD; 110, Les Palenik/AD; 111 (UP), Raymond Mendez/age fotostock; 111 (LO), Kurit afshen/SS; 112 (LO), Terrence L'Estrange/SS; **Chapter Five:** 114-115, dzultikri dzulfikti/EyeEm/AD; 116, Anke Sauerwein/Getty Images; 117 (UP), jimcumming88/AD; 117 (CTR), Hummingbird Art/AD; 117 (LO), PiggingFoto/SS; 118-119, Priyank Dhami/SS; 120-121, robertharding/AD; 122 (UP LE), Runja/SS; 122 (UP RT), Amanda Schell/SS; 122 (LO), aprison aprison/EyeEm/AD; 123 (UP LE), Nattawut Ngernsanthia/AD; 123 (UP RT), Milan Zygmunt/SS; 123 (CTR), Sandra Burm/AD; 123 (LO LE), Dave Montreuil/SS; 124 (UP), Joe/AD; 124 (LO), Lawrence/AD; 125 (UP), Michelle/AD; 125 (LO), prochym/AD; 128 (CTR), Dhritiman Mukherjee; 129 (UP), Megan Paine/AD; 129 (LO), noppharat/AD; 130 (UP), Luis César Tejo/SS; 130 (LO), Jay Ondreicka/SS; 131 (UP LE), momo5287/AD; 131 (UP RT), bennytrapp/AD; 131 (CTR RT), Vickey Chauhan/SS; 131 (LO LE), Raghu_Ramaswamy/Getty Images; 132 (LO), Nigel/AD; **Chapter Six:** 134-135, Esther van Hulsen/Stocktrek Images/Alamy Stock Photo; 136-137, Mark P. Witton/Carnegie Museum/Science Source; 138, Mark Garlick/Science Source; 139 (UP), Daniel Eskridge/AD; 139 (CTR RT), AlienCat/AD; 139 (LO), Esther van Hulsen/Stocktrek Images/Alamy Stock Photo; 140, Franco Tempesta; 141 (UP), slowmotiongli/AD; 141 (CTR), dottedyeti/AD; 141 (LO), panupol/AD; 142, warpaintcobra/AD; 143 (UP), Sergey Krasovskiy/Getty Images; 143 (UP CTR), Lewisroland/AD; 143 (LO CTR), John Conway/Science Source; 143 (LO), Lou-Foto/Alamy Stock Photo; 144, Jose Antonio Penas/Science Source; 145 (UP), Reimar/AD; 145 (CTR), MuhammadHamizan/AD; 145 (LO), Doug Perrine/Nature Picture Library; 146 (UP), warpaintcobra/AD; 146 (CTR), Pincarel/SS; 146 (LO), Worakit Sirijinda/SS; 147 (UP), YuRi Photolife/SS; 147 (CTR LE), CSP_Bepsimage/age fotostock; 147 (CTR RT), Marques/SS; 147 (car), Tatiana Popova/SS; 147 (LO), thaloengsak/AD; 148 (LO), slowmotiongli/AD; **Chapter Seven:** 150-151, Georgette Douwma/Getty Images; 152-153, Ken Griffiths/AD; 153 (inset), Sanoj Wijayasekara; 154-155, F.Rubino/SS; 155 (inset), Anup Shah/Nature Picture Library; 156-157, Frank Glaw; 157 (inset), Mariano Sayno/Getty Images; 159 (LO RT), Thomas Marent/Minden Pictures; 160-161, Westend61/Getty Images; 164-165, Michael Patrick O'Neill/Alamy Stock Photo; 165 (inset), Tomas Kotouc/SS; 166-167, mgkuijpers/AD; 167 (inset), Sanoj Wijayasekara; 168 (LE), dave stamboulis/Alamy Stock Photo; 168 (RT), KQ Ferris/AD; 169 (UP), Buddy Mays/Alamy Stock Photo; 169 (CTR LE), fauzan maududdin/EyeEm/AD; 169 (CTR RT), Kjeld Friis/AD; 169 (LO), creativenature.nl/AD; 170 (LO), Milan/AD; **Chapter Eight:** 172-173, ArtushFoto/AD; 174-175, Matthijs Kuijpers/Dreamstime; 176 (LO LE), ABCDstock/AD; 176-177 (UP), Grigory Bruev/AD; 177 (UP RT), shota/AD; 178, Willem Van Zyl/AD; 179 (UP), Philip Melgren; 179 (CTR LE), Daniel Heuclin/Nature Picture Library; 179 (CTR RT), slowmotiongli/AD; 179 (LO), I Wayan Sumatika/AD; 182 (UP), Tomas Diagne; 182 (LO), Renz Perez for Masungi Georeserve; 183 (UP RT), Panduka de Silva; 183 (CTR LE), M. Bruny; 183 (LO LE), Ingo Arndt; 184, white78/AD; 185 (UP), arkanex/Getty Images; 185 (CTR), galitskaya/AD; 185 (LO), Sidekick/AD

To Mum, Naomi, and Nilu—three amazing women who gave me and continue to give me all the support to follow my passions —R.S.

Compilation copyright © 2023 National Geographic Partners, LLC

All rights reserved. Reproduction of the whole or any part of the contents without written permission from the publisher is prohibited.

NATIONAL GEOGRAPHIC and Yellow Border Design are trademarks of the National Geographic Society, used under license.

Since 1888, the National Geographic Society has funded more than 14,000 research, conservation, education, and storytelling projects around the world. National Geographic Partners distributes a portion of the funds it receives from your purchase to National Geographic Society to support programs including the conservation of animals and their habitats. To learn more, visit natgeo.com/info.

For more information, visit nationalgeographic.com, call 1-877-873-6846, or write to the following address:

National Geographic Partners, LLC
1145 17th Street NW
Washington, DC 20036-4688 U.S.A.

For librarians and teachers: nationalgeographic.com/books/librarians-and-educators

More for kids from National Geographic: natgeokids.com

National Geographic Kids magazine inspires children to explore their world with fun yet educational articles on animals, science, nature, and more. Using fresh storytelling and amazing photography, *Nat Geo Kids* shows kids ages 6 to 14 the fascinating truth about the world—and why they should care. **natgeo.com/subscribe**

For rights or permissions inquiries, please contact National Geographic Books Subsidiary Rights: bookrights@natgeo.com

Designed by Sanjida Rashid

Library of Congress Cataloging-in-Publication Data

Names: Somaweera, Ruchira, author. I Drimmer, Stephanie Warren, author.
Title: The ultimate book of reptiles / Ruchira Somaweera with Stephanie Warren Drimmer.
Description: Washington, D.C. : National Geographic Kids, [2023] I Includes index. I Audience: Ages 8-12 I Audience: Grades 4-6
Identifiers: LCCN 2022023763 I ISBN 9781426373732 (hardcover) I ISBN 9781426373824 (reinforced library binding)
Subjects: LCSH: Reptiles--Juvenile literature.
Classification: LCC QL644.2 .S698 2023 I DDC 597.9--dc23/eng/20220630
LC record available at https://lccn.loc.gov/2022023763

The publisher would like to thank the team that made this book possible: Ariane Szu-Tu, editor; Sarah J. Mock, senior photo editor; Danny Meldung, photo research; Alicia Klepeis, fact-checker; Supun Jayaweera, dinosaur expert; Alix Inchausti, senior production editor; and David Marvin and Lauren Sciortino, associate designers.

Printed in South Korea
23/SPSK/1